The Little Red Book
for SALES MANAGERS

**The simplest, most effective One-on-One
Sales Management tool ever created**

John Golde

Published by
LITERARY PRESS
Newport Beach, California

ISBN No.: 978-0-9764-765-4-2

Author: John Golde

Table of Contents

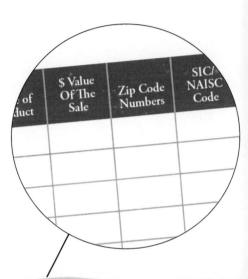

There are 19 columns to the TTR — each one will allow you to guide, lead and mentor your sales reps to increase sales, exceed quotas and drastically reduce turnover.

	$ Value Of The Sale	Zip Code Numbers	SIC/ NAISC Code

Date Became a Prospect	Source of the Lead	Name of Account	Title of Decision Maker	Type of Product	$ Value of the Sale	Zip Code Numbers	SIC/ NAICS Code	Survey Date Completed	

INTRODUCTION
The One-on-One Sales Management System

osal Date	Proposal Preparation & Review	Date For Follow Up	Date For Follow Up	Date For Follow Up	Forcasted Closing Date	Date Closed	Install And Training Date	Date Of Referral

This book was written for sales managers in every conceivable industry and profession. No matter what you make or what service you offer, sales are always based on One-on-One relationships.

My proprietary Triple Tracker Reporting System (TTR) is a potent yet very simple method that empowers you, the new or seasoned sales manager to *lead* rather than *sell.* It gives you the tools you need to do what you can do best: motivate and create a performance-based culture within your company. It allows you and your sales reps to manage prospects (no one ever closed a suspect). With my One-on-One Sales Management system, you can motivate your reps to succeed by teaching them to motivate themselves.

This system is based on common sense and over 40 years of sales and management success. It is also based on my experience in a variety of industries with a vast array of customer cultures. It is like nothing you have ever used before…

…yet it boils down to one electronic page you can manipulate and print at will.

If you are currently using existing dated time and profit worn techniques, you are most likely allowing redundancy, complications, time intensity, and high costs to hinder your efforts and that's something no self-respecting sales manager wants. However, since that is the way "business as usual" has worked for decades, you may simply be following in the footsteps of the manager you replaced, and that would be a mistake.

At the heart of this One-on-One management system is the Triple Tracker Report. The TTR is a process not just a single document, one that any high school student could easily comprehend and put into daily practice within minutes. Therefore, the true magic of my system is in how you use it and you will learn how to do that in this book along with many other strategies that all seasoned high performance sales manager's use.

If you are new to the management position in sales, you know the feeling you get when you ask yourself why the sales reps reporting to you are not as good as you were. Usually that has meant treating your sales force as a team, which is okay for a softball coach, but not with your sales reps.

The relationship between you and your sales reps must be a One-on-One proposition. Increasing your company's sales is NOT a team effort, at least not in the traditional sense. Each of your reps has a unique personality and style so it is up to you to lead and guide them accordingly One-on-One.

The traditional forms of team building in sales are non-productive by nature. I will explain all this of course as we go, but understand this now, the Triple Tracker Reporting System (TTR) will allow you to raise the bar on your sales figures to levels you've never thought possible. The Triple Tracker System to facilitate One-on-One Sales Management is going to empower you to be more effective than you have ever been. Remember, managing is not selling; selling is what your sales reps are supposed to be doing. You cannot do the selling for them. Instead, you must be the leader who motivates, drives, holds these individuals accountable and ultimately is responsible for their success. And now you will have the proper tools to do that. Of course an introduction wouldn't be complete without you knowing at least a little about me, what my credentials are, why my 40+ years of sales and sales management experience are so important, and why I want you to have my simple but powerful system.

John Golde

Within days of disembarking from the ship that brought my mother and me to the Brooklyn Navy Yard, my mother was working full time as a nurse in Colchester, Connecticut. We were lucky she'd proven, to the immigration officials she already had a promised full time job so we did not have to go through the typical induction process; we were sponsored legal immigrants from a war-ravaged Europe. I will never forget seeing the Statue of Liberty for the first time standing proudly on Ellis Island as if she were protecting not only the harbor, but all of America.

As a nine-year-old boy from Latvia who spoke no English, (my mother didn't either), our first weeks in this new country were both exhilarating and bewildering but with all my excitement and fears, I managed to go to school the next day, learned how to hit a ball with a stick at recess and within weeks had a pretty good handle on the language, at least enough to get along with my friends and do my studies.

We had left Latvia while the war was still raging and withdrew to Germany when the Russians started coming for the second time (the first time they came, they had taken thousands to Siberia).

Soon after we left in 1944, most of Europe was in a state of controlled chaos. The British, Americans and Russians were fighting over who got what chunk of land or territory. We had no choice but to run. We walked at night hiding from the Russian troops all the way to Frankfurt from Weimar where we entered into a Displaced Person's Camp. We stayed there until we were able to secure a sponsor in 1949 for my mom in the United States.

To this day, I thank her for choosing America; she had choices of several countries that were vying for her job skills as a nurse but was adamant on going to the United States, which she knew offered the most opportunities (mostly for me, I think).

Immigrants tend to gather where there is a large representation of people from the same country and so we finally wound up in Chicago by way of Connecticut. Our way station was an orphanage in Toledo, Ohio where my mom once again worked as a nurse and I stayed with the orphan boys.

Looking back at those critical six years of experiences from war torn Europe and finally to Chicago, I realize they contributed greatly to my life-long drive to succeed.

I cannot remember a time when I didn't have a job.

At the age of eleven, I created my first job, delivering groceries from in front of an A&P store for people who didn't have cars. Of course, I had no idea what an entrepreneur was, but I later learned. I had just observed the problems people were having and came up with a simple solution. I would load people's groceries on to my Red Flyer Wagon and then pull it back with them to their homes.

It was 1950. My little venture soon grew as I used my newfound wealth to buy several other Red Flyer Wagons. I rented these out to other young kids as my service continued to grow. Of course, I still hauled my own loads, but I was effectively cloning myself and charging the walk home customers as well as charging a small wagon rental fee to my sub-contractors. I guess I was the original Uber.

Looking back now, that was the very beginnings of my love for mentoring as well. I not only provided earnings for my subs, I taught them everything I knew about working with customers (such as it was then) and I loved that part of my job as well.

I could write an entire book on the jobs I had growing up; as many of you could, I'm sure. From being a theater usher, having a paper route, mowing lawns, washing dishes, working in retail, stocking ladies hats, you name it, I did just about everything a young boy was legally able to do.

I was always working either for myself or for others and by saving most of my money, I was later able to put myself through college at the University of Illinois, then went on to get my MBA in Marketing at the Kellogg School of Management at Northwestern University.

During those earliest years living with my mother, I learned English and read voraciously. I always made it a point to get good grades and to aim for success in everything I did. I know that spirit came from my mother who managed to start her own business and open a shop to do facial massages in downtown Chicago where she catered to a cadre of wealthy customers. She was very successful, so I was lucky; I had her self-starter, self-sufficient DNA.

In addition, those six formative years allowed me to overcome my fears and were the foundation for independent critical thinking and the roadmap for success in business that I have enjoyed my entire life.

Before I went to college, I served three years in the U.S. Army in Germany (ironically), where the culture exposed me to a completely new world of possibilities and helped to further shape my goals and me. I quickly learned to observe and emulate successful people and made sure I always avoided the mistakes of the unsuccessful, which meant studying them as much as the successful ones.

Since my college days until the present (2016), I've only worked for three companies and even then, I was always what we called an "intra-preneur (nearly autonomous within the company), the guy who would never be the President or CEO because he was too busy selling something or managing sales people One-on-

One. I was always the one who questioned everything or asked, "What if?" "Why not?"

I don't want to bore you with a resume but it is important for you to understand at least some of my business/life experiences and to know that the man who wrote the book you just paid for, has had more than 40 years of successful sales and marketing experience.

My One-on-One sales management system is built upon all of those real life, hands on experiences not only in sales and marketing, but with the drivers of all corporate success—the Customers (which you'll note is always capitalized in this book for good reasons you'll discover shortly).

My first job after graduating from the University of Illinois was as a buyer for part of a team that equipped the Phase I Building of the Chicago Circle Campus of the University of Illinois. That gave me a great deal of experience dealing with sales reps from a variety of businesses including foreign suppliers until 1966.

I then spent a year with a company that later merged with McCormick (spices). Before there were computers, there were punch card systems, which I used to compile customer data and to assign SIC codes to Customers. I was also involved in the company's first marketing efforts as well as being instrumental in pulling this new department together with the sales department to help each other. That is when I became interested in sales and realized I had a real knack for it.

During these first few years of employment, I also finished my MBA at the Kellogg School of Management.

In 1968, I joined Xerox as a "Copier Duplicator" sales rep and quickly earned top honors. Eventually,

I was the top sales producer in my territory and my discovery of a highly successful application contributed to the development of the first Xerox reduction copier.

My love for what I called, "Applications selling" started when I realized the power I had when I gave the Customer solutions that generated more revenue and profits. I quickly realized that was what made the sale in addition to coming up with creative new ways to use our products for other departments within their company they hadn't thought of; anything that would contribute to the bottom line. That often meant looking at my various products or services in very inventive new ways, applications that the prospect had never thought of aside from copying and of course, I applied that thinking to all new prospects as well. I've always known it's easier and far cheaper to keep an existing customer happy than it is to go find new ones.

In 1969, I was promoted to International Manager at Cheshire Inc., a company Xerox had just acquired.

Because of my MBA and a fluency in German, I was able to work well with the European culture where most of their dealers were located.

Within two years, I was promoted to Commercial Market Development Manager where I launched a new product for a finishing capability that provided Cheshire with a new product and Xerox with a new application for their innovative Docutech Copier Duplicator.

The following year, I began to pursue a sales career with Cheshire in Field Management for the newly formed Dallas branch. I was able to cover 43% of the U.S. with only four sales reps and with my marketing experience was able to bring us to the number one Branch status in the U.S.

From there, I became the District Manager in New York responsible for the three largest branches in the company.

In 1974, I was promoted back to Cheshire Head-quarters where, as Marketing manager I was responsible for Worldwide Marketing helping form a joint venture between Cheshire and Rank Xerox U.S.S.R. From 1975 to 1978, I was the National Sales Manager with 156 field sales personnel where I helped the company grow sales ten-fold in annual revenues.

Finally, in 1978, I left Xerox and joined a company called GBC Inc., to head up a new venture in National Account selling which involved implementing a new sales training program for 56 sales/branch managers. It was the first time they had ever received formal training. I also developed the first Direct Response vehicle by creating a catalog. That idea helped Dick Uline to launch the highly successful Uline Corporation, a multi-billion dollar privately owned firm that is still successfully using a catalog today as its main marketing tool.

For the next 30 years, I worked for GBC as a Regional VP of Sales and VP of the Dealer Division. In the latter position, I had the good fortune to become an intra-preneur within that division while having the total support of a Fortune 1000 company. In other words, I was given free rein to create, manage, and produce results—a business within the business. In this role, I was exposed to the constant challenges of getting things done through the voluntary co-operation of hundreds of dealers worldwide. They did not work for GBC, however we earned our share of voice through constantly helping them to meet and exceed their objectives. We provided assistance in so many ways that we earned their trust, respect and business by staying focused on a message that answered two questions:

1. What's in it for them?
2. What are their chances for success?

Date Became a Prospect	Source of the Lead	Name of Account	Title of Decision Maker	Type of Product	$ Value of the Sale	Zip Code Numbers	SIC/ NAICS Code	Survey Date Completed	C

CHAPTER ONE

The Mission of *One-on-One Sales Management*

osal Date	Proposal Preparation & Review	Date For Follow Up	Date For Follow Up	Date For Follow Up	Forcasted Closing Date	Date Closed	Install And Training Date	Date Of Referral

Don't fool yourself. This book isn't about just a simple digital document or printed page, though that certainly is a sublime aspect of One-on-One management. The magic is in how you use it along with all the other powerful insights I am going to give you with respect to each and every entry on the TTR. The anecdotes and true examples I'll be giving you all illustrate one or more "hidden" ways to use each of the 19 columns of information you will help your reps capture—things you probably have not even thought of. At first glance, these columns may look oversimplified, but nothing could be further from the realities of the stories behind each piece of information.

This book is a series of stories within a greater story that will give you the power to change your professional life and your company's future almost immediately and so, what looks like a single page of headers and columns you'll see momentarily, are actually *the keys to the kingdom of sales management, management wisdom and success.* It is filled with my own rules of success based on over 40 years of sales achievements and wealth building with some of the best-known, highly respected companies in America.

Here is the first and foremost rule:

Golde's Rule #1:

Every corporate organization chart in America must be redrawn! It must be a Corporate Organization Chart with the Customer at the peak and the CEO, Chairman and even the shareholders at the bottom!

Not many corporate organizational charts have the Customer at the top. We must remember, nothing happens in business until someone sells or buys something, so doesn't it make sense for the Chairman, the CEO and the Sales Managers to support the sales representative <u>who is the first and foremost point of contact with our Customers?</u>

GOLDE'S RULE #1 THE CUSTOMER RULES

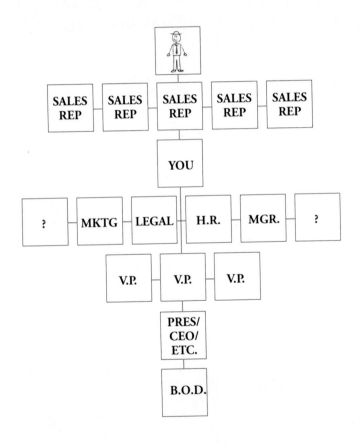

I know it sounds trite; we always "say" we are putting the Customer first, but are we really? The answer is no; in most cases an unequivocal NO. My years of experience in small, medium, and large companies taught me that *the highest levels of management and ownership need to drive and support the sales representative who is closest to the Customer.* Most corporations today are set up to serve various individuals within the company—not to serve the Customer.

In this book, I will show you exactly what that really means. I will show you how the TTR forces the sales rep to be accountable to you, the sales manager, and to the Customer and why this is a symbiotic relationship. There are three entities involved in this process: The Customer, the sales rep, and you, the sales manager. All of these interactions are One-on-One using the TTR.

If you are going to literally create, manage and mentor a winning sales representative, and in turn build sales (and by that, I mean sales and/or referrals from those sales that keep on giving for years) you must absorb this fact to your very core.

The major focus of this book is to teach you how to use the TTR to drive the kinds of sales you never dreamed possible, to make your reps self sufficient, to push them to exceed quotas and to drastically reduce turnover.

Here are some of the benefits:

- TTR allows you to lead rather than sell. It shows you how to multiply your efforts through your sales reps in a highly effective manner
- The TTR creates a performance based culture
- TTR eliminates the need for extensive control through Call Reports
- It completely frees you up to lead One-on-One because you and your reps will no longer waste time entering data collected that leads to nowhere

- The TTR is simply a one view, one source on one page key that drives accountability
- There is no software required other than to download the TTR as a PDF (free on my web site at: www.littleredsalesbook.com)
- TTR focuses on managing qualified prospects by establishing clear guidelines for each sales rep to reach the closing stage, not managing *suspects* or *contacts* that rarely produce any revenues. We used to call this, "Keeping the funnel half full." As you'll see, if your sales reps are continually recording 3 to 5 or more real prospects per month in the TTR (or whatever number of prospects and time period you determine is your goal), you will be seeing increased sales very soon. The steps in making a sale, as outlined in this book, consist of a process that if followed will yield outstanding results. I guarantee it or I will return the money you spent on this book!

Date Became a Prospect	Source of the Lead	Name of Account	Title of Decision Maker	Type of Product	$ Value of the Sale	Zip Code Numbers	SIC/ NAICS Code	Survey Date Completed	C

CHAPTER TWO

Out with the old. In with the new.

sal ate	Proposal Preparation & Review	Date For Follow Up	Date For Follow Up	Date For Follow Up	Forcasted Closing Date	Date Closed	Install And Training Date	Date Of Referral

We have really lost our edge as sales managers because most of us are working with sales reporting and communications systems as old as carbon paper. They are tedious, non-productive data entry exercises that provide almost no tools or strategies that you, as the sales manager, can use effectively. By effectively, I mean identifying real prospects (not suspects or contacts) among other things, and then drive actual sales, and more of them.

For the last few decades with the advent of all the technology that now "serves" us, we have completely lost the prime driver of sales—a One-on-One relationship between sales managers and their reps and the sales reps and their Customers. What you need is a simple tool to facilitate that relationship and communication, not more technology, repetition and distance between you and your reps. Perhaps most importantly though, the lack of a One-on-One based relationship ends up creating more layers between upper management from the actual source of the company's wealth and happiness—buying Customers, repeat Customers.

Automation, hi-tech, academic, and corporate "double talk," and endless meetings that achieve little, have created a misdirected environment where other priorities take precedent over the one and only truly important point: you and your sales reps must generate sales in order to generate profits that are always expected by all the players including: top management, suppliers, shareholders, other employees. These people however, rarely see or talk to their Customers. Your sales reps are the true face of your company, the first line of communication, the ones who most intimately understand the Customer—or at least they should!

You cannot continue to waste precious time and resources filling in outdated weekly call reports that tell you nothing.

You cannot continue to manage without holding your reps accountable by insisting on predetermined objectives and then measuring the results.

You cannot lead without trust.

You must lead One-on-One.

I have already given you Golde's Rule #1 on page 26? However, the Customer is so important to the entire corporation, it is well worth repeating that the organizational chart must have the Customer at the top. That is because corporate America is structured like a principality wherein each prince is an indepen-dent fiefdom with his or her own structure and ego that rarely collaborate with each other. You may not be able to redraw your company's organizational chart, but you can redraw the one for your sales department, which would be far simpler: the Customer at the top, then your sales reps who are in direct contact with those Customers and then you.

Placing yourself at the bottom does not mean you aren't important. On the contrary, as in the case of the CEO, you are the leader, the mentor, the guide. As any great CEO will agree, leadership and effectiveness begin by setting examples and delegating the right responsibilities to the right people and then managing that through the organization—in your case, your reps. Leadership is about mentoring but it is also about mentoring the right people who have the talent and the ability to listen and learn quickly and to take initiative whenever possible. This is your responsibility.

With my One-on-One Sales Management System, everyone communicates and collaborates directly and individually, and the focus of everyone in the enterprise is on the Customer, the end user, the one responsible for *everyone's* jobs.

The relationship between you and your sales reps is very much like that of a fighter squadron of combat pilots. Yes, there is a team of players and there is a "leader" and they must work in unison (for the good of the company so to speak). However, in a combat squadron, each of the pilots is also a leader, self-sufficient to a significant degree. In other words, each individual pilot must take the initiative often and, at the same time, be working for the common good of the squadron. Much of what each pilot does, is based upon being a leader within the group.

In your group of sales reps, there is a similar dynamic occurring only in this case, if there is an enemy, it's consistently failing to meet quotas, high turnover rates and worse.

In this group, you must lead all your reps toward the same common goal—increase sales and referrals, and you do that One-on-One on a daily basis. Using the TTR allows you to lead, mentor and manage in the most personalized manner possible. When you are leading in this manner, each of your sales reps whether that's three or three hundred, will be microcosms of the entire sales enterprise you lead. In using the TTR as your primary communication tool with each rep, you are customizing their efforts to reach out to their particular customers in a way that cannot be duplicated with any other process.

So many corporations in America today don't have a clue what their Customers are truly feeling and thinking and there are marketing departments that rarely talk One-on-One with the sales department. In reality, marketing should constantly be asking sales, "What do our Customers want? What do they like/dislike about our products? Where do you find your best Customers?" And other questions along these lines. Your sales reps are the key and the conduit to those answers!

Here are a few other thoughts you and your marketing department can work on in a One-on-One manner:

- How do we help our Customers make money? Does our Customer make money with our products?
- How can we help our Customers make more money?
- How can we help our Customers make money in the future?
- Do we measure how much more money we have helped your Customer make over a period of time?
- Do we measure how much more money our Customers make doing business with us relative to competition?

These are all powerful questions with potentially powerful answers if you and your marketing department ask them, get them answered and then measure the results of the changes you make. If you do that, you will be well on your way to increased sales and revenues.

As most seasoned sales managers know, it is imperative to keep your ear to the ground, meaning listening to your Customers directly, asking them what your company can do better, faster, more economically. That One-on-One conversation must be relayed all the way up, or in this case, "down" the chain of command to upper management. Your Customers know more about how they use your products or services than you do. You must listen to them and then put those insights, concerns or kudos into practice.

We've all experienced poor Customer service whether that was in a restaurant, a large retail store or just about anywhere we all interact with each other and money is involved. So that you and your company don't fall into this trap, I would advise you to convey to your sales reps Golde's Rule #1 but to take it a step further, I would add, that incredibly good Customer service begins in the hearts and brains of your reps, those who have the most intimate contact with your Customers. They must believe down to their core, that incredible Customer service is what sets your company apart from all the others. A great concept in sales has always been to "add value" to every transaction. In other words, take the extra steps that the client never expected of you.

We can never lose sight of the fact that nothing happens until your sales reps sell something and that goes for the largest to the smallest most diverse manufacturing and/or service business. That is why, your sales rep is the point man for the entire company in many ways, and it is why, with my TTR system, you must maintain the highest degree of One-on-One communications with each of them.

If, your reps do not feel this way and your Customers are "put off" by one of your rep's attitude or performance, they have powerful recourses in today's internet driven world—Yelp, among others will very quickly ferret out the losers and it will be painful to your bottom line not to mention the lack of any referrals.

This sword that will harm your bottom line has two edges however, you can use Yelp and others of similar format to your advantage. Ask your satisfied customers to go to Yelp and write a good review about their experiences with your sales rep and your company. Begin to build that very public face of trust, dependability, great service and all the other assets you know your company offers by enlisting the help of Yelp yourself.

In his book, *Moneyball*, we meet Billy Beane, General Manager of the Oakland As baseball team. He realized that if he were to have a chance to beat the big market teams, he had to do something different, break from tradition, challenge conventional wisdom, and apply a new methodology when examining players and their talents.

He found that the things that were thought to be most important such as home runs, runs batted in and batting averages had a poor correlation to wins and losses. What really counted was the percentage of a player's plate appearances when the player reached first. On defense, the standard fielding percentage was replaced by how many runners were being put out when they hit the ball and therefore were prevented from reaching first base.

The TTR in this book can be called the "Salesball" system in that it refocuses the sales organization on their main job and that is, to close sales and provide the Customers with exceptional service.

Everyone depends on the sales force to bring in the most important factor to growth and survival of the business. Yet in many sales departments, the following exists:

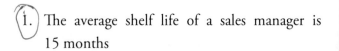 1. The average shelf life of a sales manager is 15 months

2. Four out of ten sales reps will lose their jobs in less than a year

3. An average of 27% of sales reps will not even produce enough to cover their employment costs!

In the next chapter, I am going to explain the single most important document or digital page your organization will ever use to increase sales.

Most sales managers are promoted from within as a reward for their excellent sales results. Unfortunately, far too often, the one who was the star sales person now has a completely different mission—meeting and exceeding quotas through their sales reps.

If you are the type of sales manager described above, you might have already become frustrated with your reps. Do you find yourself exasperated with your reps because they can't do what you always thought was so easy? As this type of situation grows worse day by day (and it does all across corporate America), the new manager is often demoted or reassigned, which often means he or she leaves the company—truly a lose-lose situation not only for the corporation, but for the Customers. The company has lost its best salesperson and potentially brilliant manager and may quite possibly lose sales as a result of that vacuum.

My One-on-One Management System changes all that. Now you can readily understand why your reps aren't as good as you were and then set about changing whatever deficiencies exist immediately.

Along with unnecessary technology and outdated weekly call reports, building "teams" (one of the benchmarks of the "old way") is another hurdle that hinders sales. Team building in a group of reps with varying degrees of experience and maturity is not effective (blasphemy in most corporate cultures) but true. Only

One-on-One management really works. You can have a winning team of sales reps, but that all begins with a singular relationship with one human being at a time, not in a group.

Many sales managers try to build comfort zones (however indirectly or inadvertently) to make their reps dependent on them rather than developing them to be independent of them, which is what truly leads to growth.

With my TTR, you can provide direction like the: Who, What, Why, Where and the When's of selling. You will be working at a much higher level of effectiveness providing leadership to your reps in the "selling process" not tiresome data entry routines.

As the new sales manager, or even the tenured one, your job does not consist of making sales calls and getting in to see the right decision maker; instead it is to transfer your vital skills to the sales reps one at a time. In a manner of speaking, you are "cloning" yourself by leading and managing and mentoring.

With the TTR as your primary tool, you will become a front line manager with key information at your fingertips. You will be constantly focused on the success of that rep. You'll be able to communicate clearly and quickly and you'll be able to use situational management strategies customized for each individual rep to transfer your knowledge and experience to them (the things that made you a star in sales).

Date Became a Prospect	Source of the Lead	Name of Account	Title of Decision Maker	Type of Product	$ Value of the Sale	Zip Code Numbers	SIC/ NAICS Code	Survey Date Completed	

CHAPTER THREE

The Triple Tracker Report and Sales Management System

sal ate	Proposal Preparation & Review	Date For Follow Up	Date For Follow Up	Date For Follow Up	Forcasted Closing Date	Date Closed	Install And Training Date	Date Of Referral

Before I get into the specifics of the TTR, I want to tell you what makes it such a powerful tool. On subsequent pages, I will break out each column with graphic and discuss how each works, but for now, I'm jumping ahead a little bit by using Column 1 as an example. The Triple Tracker form will only list prospects, not time wasting suspects.

There are four requirements that must be met to be a prospect:

1. Defined need for your product or service
2. The decision maker identified (extremely important as there are an average of 5.4 potential Decision Makers in a B2B environment in many corporations today and many more that "want to be" the Decision Makers but in fact, end up wasting your reps valuable time)
3. Is the necessary budget available

4. Will the sale take place in an acceptable time frame, which will vary industry by industry

In order to be considered valid, a prospect must be one who makes the decisions, understands the budget, and is the one who expresses a need for your product or service, and will be adding this product or service within an acceptable time period used for expected closing date. As you know, there is a world of difference between this individual and a contact.

In order to be entered into the TTR as a prospect, the above characteristics must be in place. This is important because 70% of what a sales rep calls a prospect is many times just hope and/or anticipation (a suspect), more than a potential sale.

As the previous star sales person in your company, you know that very few suspects are transformed into prospects. Qualifying suspects or contacts into prospects begins with filling out the TTR honestly. This saves a lot of lost time and heartache later and always leaves the rep free to devote quality time to only those who are qualified prospects. This one fact, as expressed with this simple form should be your major training focus, One-on-One. This usually represents a culture change in the company and as with all changes, you can expect some resistance. The severity of enduring the culture change will be directly associated with the Sales Manager's ability to help the sales rep add qualified prospects to the TTR immediately.

By simply reading your rep's TTR, you will see how many prospects are being added and at what frequency —the prospect is the driving force. The red flag will be when you see that no new prospects are being added.

I suggest keeping suspects on a separate TTR form; their information can then be transferred easily to the main report when they become prospects. How do you know that the date entered in the TTR column ("Date became a prospect) actually means this contact is a prospect? By talking One-on-One with your sales rep and asking the above questions just outlined.

You shouldn't care about suspects except when a sales rep starts waving a red flag in your face by suddenly adding an unusual amount of suspects to fill in as prospects to his TTR. These would of course be contacts that don't qualify with the above questions being answered to you by your rep satisfactorily— One-on-One. Then, you should start to look at the role suspects play in that rep's overall prospecting activity. The TTR only manages the process; it doesn't qualify leads for you or the reps. You must insure that what your reps "think" is a prospect, truly fits the definition. Now stop for a moment. Look at the outtake from the complete TTR on the next page, just the first column: Date became a prospect.

What do you see entered there? <u>A date, a simple
date.</u> All of the above information and some to follow
begin with that one date. However, it isn't just a date in
a column—it is the keys to the kingdom of increased
sales. Everything begins with this simple date and
column. What begins? Your ability to lead and
mentor One-on-One. As this TTR begins to fill, you
will find that you've engaged with each of your sales
reps many times One-on-One with a simple question:
Why is this a prospect and not a suspect among other
pieces of conversation that will guide your rep and give
you constant and immediate control over his or her
next moves. Note the next column, Lead Source is just
as simple, only that one isn't a date. (More on that in
a minute).

Date Became a Prospect	Source of the Lead	Name of Account	Title of Decision Maker	Type of Product	$ Value Of The Sale	Zip Code Numbers	SIC/ NAICS Code	Surv Da Comp

While I have only shared a brief overview of the first two columns, I want to share the total overview of the keys that drive the TTR system:

1. Recognizes the need for One-on-One Management

2. Effective communications due to visibility

3. Focus on need for qualified prospects

4. Ten sales reps managed with ten TTR sheets

   (Note: these TTR sheets are kept in digital form.) You can create a folder for each rep but that's it. Either the rep closes a sale, or once a quarter you have a One-on-One meeting where you and the rep delete any prospects that didn't close. A rep cannot delete a prospect until you mutually agree to do so. It is amazing how in today's world so many of what we called prospects at one time suddenly just disappear mysteriously. *Accountability is achieved through declaring a prospect and then making a major effort by everyone in the sales and marketing department to insure that the prospect converts to a sale. Of course, there will be prospects that don't close, but then you, the sales manager will have a hand in declaring them dead! They no longer continue to "linger" as true prospects raising false hopes.)*

Proposal Date	Proposal Presentation & Review	Date For Follow Up	Date For Follow Up	Date For Follow Up	Forecasted Closing Date	Date Closed	Install And Training Date	Date Of Referral

5. Create a folder for digital info to store pages showing closed sales They either close, go back to suspect status or are simply eliminated with the agreement of both you and sales reps. This is a vital step! The closed page will focus on the successes and nothing else and can represent a goldmine for applications information

6. You, the sales manager, manage all the steps to the sales process to closing AND follow up. The sales rep simply enters a date when the activity in that column is completed. There will only be dates to enter but of course, you can make your own notes in whatever manner you choose

7. The TTR builds trust instead of corporate double talk and too much tech and academic semantics

8. Your training is always ongoing as the One-on-One sales management system is implemented on a daily basis

9. Each of the 19 steps on the TTR has a specific need and purpose that you will be implementing along with ideas on how to use these simple dates as One-on-One conversations

10. You will be forced to employ collaborative support from many areas of the company with the brilliantly simple, easy to understand ammunition you have in your hands—the filled out TTR

11. Time and weekly sales accountability reports will be eliminated. You determine what reports remain in place. Using the TTR eliminates un necessary sales time usage Creates time for the rep to sell rather than report

12. Focus is placed on prospects and it is important to remember once again, this will probably reflect a cultural change in the corporation that you will have to deal with

13. You will have a better handle on the status of each rep and each of his prospects. The word

"we" will slowly make the word "I" go away. The TTR is a "we" tool – any previous tools used are "them" directed at and the sole responsibility of the sales rep without having any commitment to ownership of that prospect and the value it represents to the company/firm/business

14. No binders, no pages (unless you want to file them this way) just a a simple one page digital file to fill in (Excel). You can copy mine or simply go to my website at: www.littleredsalesbook.com

How to use all the columns on the TTR Report?

To start with, I might make a suggestion: in lieu of weekly calls or other types of reports that stress accountability versus an effective means for you to implement One-on-One Management, the sales reps might keep all their suspects on a separate TTR type of a report to make it easy for the sales rep to just transfer the initial data to the TTR that you will be reviewing once the suspect becomes a prospect. This will allow the sales rep to have the suspects organized and ready for review with you as might be required.

(Note: The first nine columns require entry regarding Customer profile, which might be easily transferrable from data that the business will require. After the first eight Columns the only other Column that needs to be filled is the forecasted close date because between the date of when a prospect was added and the forecasted closing date lies the battlefield on the which the sales process will play out the game.)

I should stress that especially for new reps the direction provided by the TTR for their activities is critical. Too many reps are left to sink or swim alone like I was. You can provide the transition to my story.

This story stresses the idea that for new reps, the direction provided by the TTR for their activities is critical!

As a rookie sales person with an MBA I was having real second thoughts about what I was doing working a starter territory on the South side of Chicago which was dominated by the Main Produce terminal, wide variety of freight companies, gasoline storage tank farms and numerous levels of manufacturers to include the Hawthorne Works of Western Electric, however, that was a major account and not assigned to me.

I looked at all the tall office buildings of downtown Chicago and dreamed of all those large companies generating Xerox copies by the ton versus my "potential" Customer base of small railroad terminal offices—it didn't look promising. Yet the experience that I was about to have was the "best" introduction to sales I could have asked for. It gave me the opportunity to make lemonade out of lemons in a big way.

I finally realized that I was surrounded by a tremendous organization of people eager to help me achieve my plans. There was an organization standing by to help me that consisted of:

People

1. Loyal Customers who talked about the role our products played in the success of their business
2. Lost Customers who were excited about any new Xerox capability and just needed to establish a level of trust with the sales rep
3. I started probing my co-workers and even worked with them in their territories and gained valuable insights
4. I turned to every "outsider" I came into contact with and turned them into leads for my co-workers—amazing how I started receiving leads in my territory from all types of sources. (I address competitors as a source of leads in later sections of the book.)

Things taken for granted

1. I started to talk about Xerox products and services in an exciting manner
2. I carried around copies of the Xerox full page ads – what a revealing and exciting thing that was to do
3. I talked about Xerox quality, distribution and total support service that were ready to go to work for the Customer
4. Lastly, I realized that I had the best product along with a company who's reputation was the best in the industry

No wonder I got promoted to a management position (in less than a year) where I actually took a pay-cut during the initial start-up period. However, I did so knowing that I was following a plan that I had developed for myself. I still visit my old starter territory and recall the excellent foundation that I put into place through facing and overcoming challenges that every sales rep experiences when not guided by sales managers that believe and implement One-on-One management principles.

Sink or swim is not a proper procedure to be used with a new sales representative—too many sink as justified by the extremely expensive turn-over rates.

Date Became a Prospect	Source of the Lead	Name of Account	Title of Decision Maker	Type of Product	$ Value of the Sale	Zip Code Numbers	SIC/ NAICS Code	Survey Date Completed	

CHAPTER FOUR

A column-by-column tutorial

sal ate	Proposal Preparation & Review	Date For Follow Up	Date For Follow Up	Date For Follow Up	Forcasted Closing Date	Date Closed	Install And Training Date	Date Of Referral

Date Became a Prospect	Source of the Lead	Name of Account	Title of Decision Maker	Type of Product	$ Value Of The Sale

COLUMN 1 - DATE BECAME PROSPECT

This is where we get down to the systematic details of the TTR beginning with Column 1: The date the person became a prospect. I discussed this briefly in the previous chapter, but now, I'll get specific.

This prospect start date triggers the entire closing cycle and serves as a reference point for the other steps of the sales process.

You will be looking at each sales rep's TTR report often because it is easy to do and the report provides immediate transparency so you will quickly see that the addition of each new prospect has a rhythm to it. You'll

candidates to convert to prospects. What steps would make that happen? Review all existing marketing programs and product applications in terms of the present suspect list. In other words, what applications do you currently use that might be used in any of these suspect's industries? In the meantime, extra help might be needed One-on-One in the field with the sales rep.

The TTR provides transparency and direction for the sales process with a high degree of immediacy and urgency in a manner that does not exist in present systems.

The major step that takes place when a sales rep declares an account as a prospect is vital especially in today's world where recognition of the multiple process steps of a sale is so important. This is actually a corporate cultural change from the past and not everyone takes to it lightly.

In 1978, I experienced this when I changed a 300 person sales force from the responsibility of submitting a long detailed form called a weekly activity report to submitting one sheet of numbers only. This was my first attempt at what has now become this TTR system. The first thing I realized with that rudimentary form was that it helped me to control numbers easier than other data.

We would receive approximately 300 reports from the branches showing their numbers and they were then tabulated by an entry clerk simply entering the numbers on the submitted form. The numbers included: total sale, total calls made, value of the sale, total suspects added, total prospects added—it was all I needed then. As time went on and my experiences taught me new things, I added more columns and more ideas on how to use that information.

We first conducted a training session to highlight the effectiveness or productivity of this system. We also got the Branch and Regional Managers to buy into it. They in turn, held sessions with the sales reps and were able to start slowly getting each rep's commitment to the simple system. The numbers and dates entered served as red, yellow, or green flags for the sales managers.

The driving force was the manager's ability to start communicating One-on-One with each sales rep about his or her performance by using this information to open the doors of conversation and analysis of what the reps were really doing. This allowed the managers to develop plans incorporating strategies all aimed at improving the rep's ability to meet and exceed their objective through what was ultimately, prospect management.

The results were immediate. We saw significant improvements not only in total sales and profitability, but in the implementation of specific important plans for many of the reps as a direct result of the manager's having more time to manage and to deal with facts that were providing actual and true conditions that each rep was facing.

One significant outcome was in the fact that we lowered turnover of sales reps to 15% providing a direct contribution to the bottom line. Quota achieving reps are happy reps.

Date Became a Prospect	Source of the Lead	Name o f Account	Title of Decision Maker	Type of Product	$ Valu Of Th Sale

COLUMN 2 - SOURCE OF THE LEAD

You'll be familiar with the sources of the leads on the TTR such as a present Customer, a new/smart call, e-commerce, direct marketing, trade shows and events, telemarketing, special marketing promos and others as needed.

You'll glean a wealth of information from this one column alone. It will give you ideas for similar suspects/ prospects using the same source. It can easily provide direction for you to specific applications and markets to maximize the creation of smart calls versus cold calls. This information will allow you to send over exacting information to the Marketing Department asking for help in maximizing this potential.

The key to success here is the establishment of a list representing abbreviations (not dates) for each source that is easy to understand and apply and will fit in the column:

> TS Trade Show
> DM Direct Mail
> C Customer
> MKTG Marketing
> EC E-Commerce…and so on.

A quick view at the source of the lead should line up other suspects/prospects that can be developed from the same sources. If the company is an architectural firm, what other architects are located nearby? (This is where the use of SIC and NAICS codes are a God-send. See Column 7). Or, what applications could be deduced from how the architect uses your product or service for use with other existing customers or prospects?

What a simple concept; just enter the name of the source and then start getting creative—it's an idea starter. Marketing will love you, the sales manager, because they will be able to transmit factual TTR prospect information regarding effective sources and begin to see what the actual steps of the sale were for the lead they created.

I am a definite believer in leads and their sources, which play such an important part for the sales manager and the sales rep, and even marketing. However, one source of lead generation lies with the competitive or other product line sales reps. Today, we call these networking groups where a group of sales reps get together weekly and exchange a wide variety of information.

In the late 1960s, I was a rookie sales rep who capitalized on introducing the most successful new product ever, the Xerox 914 plain paper copier. As I was making calls, I had many suspects inform me that they wouldn't pay the Xerox price of $95 a month to rent the copier plus .04 cents a copy since they also had to provide the paper and the toner. They told me they would rather keep their 3M, Apeco, Kodak or Minolta copiers using a variety of coated papers vs. the plain paper copies we were providing. Intent on overcoming their objections to the Xerox System, I made contact with four competitors and we started meeting once a week for lunch. We would exchange leads. I would give them those suspects that would not order Xerox and they in turn would provide me with leads to Customers that were going for the new Xerox copiers using plain paper. It was a total win-win.

At the same time, IBM had an equally hot product in the Selectric typewriter. I made contact with the sales rep from IBM that worked in my territory and we began meeting once a week for coffee to discuss a range of topics focused on potential prospects.

This source among others became win-win situations for me in that we all were promoted within a short period of time. Are you maximizing your sales rep's networking opportunities in their territories? Something important to think about.

Date Became a Prospect	Source of the Lead	Name of Account	Title of Decision Maker	Type of Product	$ Value Of The Sale

COLUMN 3 - NAME OF THE ACCOUNT

Among other information, it is important to identify the name of the account. If the business is public, a Value Line Report should be pulled and the overall status of the company should be reviewed. (https://research.valueline.com/research#sec=libraryz)

View this information carefully so you can quickly see what type of accounts that rep is developing. Are they small, medium or large? Are they manufacturing, retail, service, other? This can tell you many things such as the potential need for developing larger accounts, or accounts in areas that are more profitable or with greater needs.

As your rep gains seniority, you can take steps to get him or her to generate prospects from larger Customers. You'll have to decide whether the rep should be exposed to some formal major account selling education or perhaps decide that teaching will be limited to field training. Remember, you are the mentor and the manager. You are dealing with this rep One-on-One and this, along with any other "education" begins with your own experiences of course.

You should also have access to a local library so that the rep can access key databases and prepare for the next sales call armed with key business information such as: what are the significant indicators as to where your product could provide solutions leading to potential profits? Yes, you can get much of this on-line however, "romancing" the research librarian is an invaluable tool. This person can be worth his or her weight in gold. Just as a note, I have the head researcher at Harper College help me often. He pulls up things for me when I am not even there.

The earlier the rep is exposed to the power of the Research Librarian and internet sources, the better. You play the key role in making this happen. The earlier the rep begins to think outside the box, the better. Creative thinking begets more creative approaches using the same product in different ways.

This is an area that you as a sales manager will contribute to as a result of adding knowledge about any of the businesses listed. For example, you might have learned that XYZ Construction just received a large contract in addition to what they had when they decided to buy the new Model ABC. Perhaps there is an opportunity to sell additional or larger sizes of equipment to them because of this purchase.

These kinds of observations about these accounts will make excellent discussion points at the upcoming

TTR review session and that is the power of the TTR—as a point of One-on-One review, discussion, tracking and measuring and whatever other ideas that a good dialogue seems to foster.

The account name is a very important requirement for you. More often than not, you will have some feel for the size of the account by the name and type. Newer sales reps will most likely list smaller to mid-size accounts because their experience and confidence level will guide them in that direction. Also, keep in mind that you never know what potential a smaller account could represent. The key is for the sales rep to learn. There is knowledge in small as well as large accounts that can be applied to either size business.

Another of my true stories starts with a small freight company along Roosevelt Road on the South side of Chicago. For several months, I was getting the proverbial objection: We simply don't have a need for a copier. As I was a new rep, I accepted that as a real objection. Little did my sales manager or I know that inside the freight forwarder quite a few people sat re-typing freight bills from various trucking firms on to their own freight bills showing the information as coming from their trucking firm.

I had not gathered enough information about what their greatest challenge was on a previous visit. Had I done that, I would have found out that typing repetitive information was quite costly.

One day, I was going through my mail and I saw a written application describing a Xerox Duplicator that was working in tandem with a Minolta reduction copier (the competition), which eliminated the need for all that retyping of freight bills.

When I discovered this, I got up the next morning at 3:00 a.m., and drove 300 miles to St. Louis and was there at 9:30 a.m. I wanted the existing Xerox sales rep to share the keys to the application with me. The owner joined our meeting and gave me an approximate percentage of profit that his firm had garnered from implementing this application. The benefits resulted from taking the inbound bill and reducing the information onto one sheet that was then transferred to the Xerox high-speed copier that contained sets of preprinted colored paper onto which the information was transferred. Every copy looked like it had been originated by this freight company—using the Minolta Copier to reduce the information in a proper format that could be transferred to the Xerox high speed copier was the key—at that time Xerox did not have a reduction capability.

Our joint capabilities resulted in replacing 20+ typists who were retyping the information from the inbound bill to the new invoice representing this firm. In addition, we replaced a very expensive set of 5 copies with inserted carbon paper—(it was difficult to read the fourth and fifth copies).

At 11:00 a.m., I was on my way back to Chicago stopping at a pay phone and calling my contact that had just said he didn't need a copier. I asked him if I could get him to gather all his key personnel there for a 5:00 p.m. meeting, which he agreed to do. My meeting with them lasted an hour and a half. At the end of it, I had an order for a Xerox Copier Duplicator. Now, I had to find the Minolta rep and meet with him the next morning. For the next two weeks, I went down Roosevelt Rd. and called on trucking and freight forwarders with the same approach.

I ended up earning the honor of top Copier Duplicator sales rep in the region and soon was entertaining product development people from Xerox who saw and brought a Copier Duplicator to market with reduction capabilities so we no longer had to pair up with Minolta.

Lessons learned: The Xerox sales rep in St. Louis had the initiative to think of how he could solve the problem that his small to mid-size Customers were facing. (It's not the size of the account, but the applications and the solutions that translate into profits that you can offer that matter.) I have always loved it when a sales person offers me solutions, especially those that bring in new sources revenues and profitability.

Date Became a Prospect	Source of the Lead	Name of Account	Title of Decision Maker	Type of Product	$ Valu Of Th Sale

COLUMN 4 - TITLE OF THE DECISION MAKER

While the actual name of the decision maker might be important and could be listed, to you, the title of the decision maker is mandatory and vital!

You've had plenty of experience and you know the importance the title plays in identifying whether the individual who has provided the information actually has the power to make a solo decision. The typical corporate decision making process today involves 5.4 people —but which one is the one your rep should be talking to? Does your rep even have an idea?)

Most self-declared Decision Makers need to

obtain several other approvals, but they won't often admit that to your rep. As we all know, many of these types like to play up the power of their role or position to sales reps. You must put your experience to work here. You absolutely must know the titles that can make decisions and you'll need to start challenging the sales rep for that information. In other words, what evidence is there to support the reps inclination? It won't take long before this process of identifying the correct prospect is almost second nature to the rep with your guidance. This simple column tells you that story by forcing you and the sales rep to discuss this subject.

My best story is that too often a sales rep completely ignores the administrative people and pays more attention to who they think is the decision maker. We know that it takes 5.4 Decision Makers to approve most purchases on average. Therefore, the guidance of an administrative person can provide regarding the areas that are usually involved in the approval process can be a great help. Always talk to the administrator (the gatekeeper) and get this information.

I did this through a "resumé" that I created for the products I sold. I used this to attract the attention of the individuals who would be part of the decision. I would send the resume that presented the product in the same manner I would in my own resume. In other words, I anthropomorphized the resume and sent it in advance along with a brief letter indicating the specific benefits for the area they were responsible for. (I turned a résumé for a human into a résumé for a product.

Today, I would send that resume and letter via Fed Ex addressed to the Decision Maker's name. The value of "getting the Decision Maker's attention" cannot be understated. Most management people are inundated with mail they never read or even open. Often a secretary or assistant trashes anything that smacks of "advertising" or unwanted solicitations. He or she is the gatekeeper for that Decision Maker and one of the best ways to get past that individual is to send your materials via Fed Ex. You can even write "Personal" on the addressing slip. In "most" cases, a Fed Ex envelope is viewed at the very least, as important and in many cases, as urgent. Either way, when the Decision Maker reads your letter and resume, he or she knows you mean business and were at least creative enough to use a different vehicle to reach out to him or her; and clever enough to create a résumé for your product.

In fact, I encourage all sales reps to use an overnight delivery service often prior to many meetings and to get those meetings in the first place. A well written, short letter announcing, thanking, providing ideas or whatever you can dream up to a prospect or an existing client shows a great deal of interest and enthusiasm on your part.

I mentioned, added value before in this book. This

is one of the ways you can demonstrate your interest in your client, his needs, his bottom line and him or her. I used to scan newspapers, magazines and in the last 20 years or so, the internet for articles or news that had some interesting or important bearing on my prospect or Customer's business, or even his or her personal life.

Not only does this often bring important information to that individual, it demonstrates quickly how much "you care" or are in a line to be a "partner" of sorts to him. He or she realizes quickly that you are "thinking" of him or her at the very least, and at its best, it shows you want to be part of the team and that you are providing information that will help him that was "never expected" of you—a powerful yet very simple gesture like this can tip the scales in your favor or keep you ingratiated at the very least.

You can create a resume for your products and I'll guarantee that you will get the approval from the other 4.4 Decision Makers your key person won't tell you about. It is paramount you arm your client with a multi-level proposal in the form of a product résumé. Don't expect him to do the selling for you, at least not until you give him all the ammunition you can. The resume should provide what the product or service will do and how other Customers of yours using it, what guarantees or warranties there are and a host of other information you can have your sales rep write up. The key attention getter is the fact that the resume is a unique approach and gets attention immediately.

Create this just as you would a human resume. For example: Keep it to one page. Keep it product or service specific. Use a lot of benefits and features. If you are selling a better mousetrap, use the name of the product as you would your own name—XYZ Mousetrap. Call attention to the product's track record, just as you would your various achievements in your own employment record.

* Benefits I provide: 24 hour hassle free operation
* I am lethal 100% of the time
* Set me down and walk away—no maintenance and only one moving part

I'm sure you get the idea. This technique helped me close many sales, but perhaps more importantly, the use of the resume earned me a nickname among many of our new Customers who began to smile and say, "Hey, it's the resume man," when I walked in their doors.

I would also encourage you to take a picture or better yet, a video on your smartphone that showed the key operational person along with the Decision Maker so that the Customer could get the story of the "miracle" we were performing with our capabilities. We would use it on the next call as an endorsement internally in that company, or with another prospect.

For the sales reps: We would make every effort to get as much exposure within a larger firm in the form of a quick story in the house organ or posting pictures, or a brochure showing the use of our products by their fellow employees.

Today's instant photo and video capabilities provide your sales rep with a great lead generator that is only limited by his or her imagination. A very quick video showing a happy customer using your product or talking about it with you in glowing terms can be a very powerful sales tool. Your sales rep only has to choose the right time in the conversation, reach into his pocket and turn on his phone and then preface the 20 second video as he turns it to his prospect.

Take this a step further and create speed dial listings of all your current and soon to be Customers. Then create a template letter or note to use in the body of all the emails you'll be sending these individuals. Send that Bcc along with the video and voila! You have just created an excellent marketing communication tool all of which took you 10 minutes.

Take this a step further and instead of watching T.V. tonight, sit down and organize your smart phone. Categorize your endorsement videos and or pictures. Then create a separate listing of all your current Customers and prospects in your contacts. Then, break that down further in your contacts to include all of the known 4.4 Decision Makers for each of these people. Bravo, you have just created the most powerful data base you'll ever use. Use it to send thank you's (a very overlooked simple edge). Use it to send endorsement pictures and videos. Use it to forward great articles you've just read about a similar business. Anytime you send a prospect or client information that they would be interested in, would increase their sales, or make their lives easier, you get Brownie points. You're showing

that you have your customer's and prospect's best interests at heart and don't just show up when you want to
make a sale—you add value to your proposition and
you exceed his or her expectations. The options are
practically endless.

There is nothing as powerful as your "mailing list"
or data base. It is worth its weight in platinum. If you
doubt me, do you think your competition wouldn't pay
dearly for that list? Further, just look at the data mining
that is going on second by second in today's internet,
social media etc. There is a reason Google, Facebook
and all the others spend millions gathering everything
they can find out about you—they want to sell
you something!!

Again, you can play a vital role in recognizing the
strength of the Decision Maker from the Location, the
Title and Function in the hierarchy of most businesses.
In most instances, you know which Sr. Management

Title will be the key player that your reps will have to concentrate on with the recognition that most decisions in larger businesses require more than one approval. You will be exploring the strength of the Decision Maker at any company due to weakness in Title as well. As an example, if his or her title were Assistant to the Assistant, you can readily see how a simple title tells a story you need to know.

The name of the person should be captured for your reference but will make little if any difference in evaluating the overall strength of the prospect. Will knowing the names Betty A., John C., William J., make any difference?

How Many Decision Makers are there?

You have to take one look at the Decision Makers title and you will know that there will be an approval matrix that can average 4.4 additional people that have to be sold. Most sales reps will indicate that they are with the right Decision Maker, but that can hardly be realistic when the average number of people involved in a B2B sale is once again, 5.4, and in most cases consensus approval has to take place. A title of Purchasing Agent, might indicate strength, but you'll only know if you talk to your rep One-on-One to investigate further.

Don't ever assume your sales reps are talking to the one and only Decision Maker because there are usually 4.4 others he may not even have accounted for. All 5.4 Decision Makers must be sold and your rep can use his initial prospect to help him or her sell to the others (more on that in a minute).

Human nature is at work on the part of both the Decision Maker and the sales rep. The Decision Maker will never admit that he can't make the decision without additional approvals, and the sales rep is afraid to attempt to go around his main contact who he thinks is the only Decision Maker. In addition, we are faced with the fear on the part of the people in the approval matrix of losing respect or credibility if they push for something that might not attract support, or if they are a part of something that doesn't turn out well.

A good number of people will not favor any change and constantly refer to the tired old saying that nobody was ever fired for buying IBM. While our insistence on preparing a proposal will be covered later, it is imperative to understand the importance of the SURVEY step early in the process.

It is very important for the sales rep to get as much information regarding the individuals that will be involved from key operational areas in order to be able to add a personal touch to eliminating personal risk. This is where you can play a key role to guide the rep in understanding that the more individuals that can be positioned as key contributors to profitability and Customer service, the more impact you will gain versus just addressing organizational risks and rewards. The TTR is the place you start!

Too often businesses are emphasizing the wrong overall values, which avoid mobilizing key approval personnel's individual contributions towards building consensus.   Numerous internal champions need to be worked with to insure that their weight brings the support needed to adopt your solution.

I know one thing for sure: do not leave the internal selling up to your sales rep's identified Decision Maker. A well-prepared proposal will go a long way toward moving the sale through the internal approval matrixes that exist in most businesses. In addition, it is important to make sure you recognize that Marketing has to be involved in knowing the need for consensus "busters" to work with the sales rep to make the case internally for your product. These "busters" can take a form ranging from: supporting case studies featuring applications information on similar processes that are providing benefits; a series of users in the industry, to facilities assessments, and site surveys.

A new era of alignment of all supporting areas with Sales has to be in place or the competition that does practice this strategy will begin to beat you to the sale.

Date Became a Prospect	Source of the Lead	Name of Account	Title of Decision Maker	Type of Product	$ Value Of The Sale

COLUMN 5 - TYPE OF PRODUCT

This information represents the obvious critical factor that identifies specific "solutions/equipment model numbers, etc.," that are going to be offered to the prospect. This column also provides another clear benefit right away: could this be a new opportunity in a new market? If the answer is yes, you have the foundation you need to begin to track this prospect through to a close. It's important to note that this will give you a powerful database of suspects to begin to develop in this new market. It allows you to alert the Marketing department so that they are able to maximize the opportunities and work with you on new ideas. You can also see which products your sales reps are favoring. Some reps have a tendency to feature certain products only or small vs. bigger capabilities. Even price can be an indicator of contact levels. Your responsibility at this point is not only to get a product sale, but also to make sure that it is the right product sale for that Customer. Think carefully about what types of products sell in certain types of territories or concentrations of companies?

To simplify this, visualize a chart with only one company such as Boeing in the left hand column. Then across the top visualize the departments: Human resources, Accounting, Administration and so on.

Let's say there are six locations at Boeing that you would list in the left column. Each of these six locations have eight similar departments and functions, which you would put across the top of your matrix. Further assume you have your products installed in three of these locations (one each in a different department). This gives you a quick reference as to what departments are using which of your products.

Your first question should be: How many of those six locations have departments that should be using your products due to the fact that you have identified an area in one location? This leaves you five potential areas to call on where you can refer to the success of your products in their own company in different locations. This makes this a very "hot" lead.

From the use of this matrix approach you have identified let's say, 15 areas that you can call on because you "understand your Customer and you can meet their existing and potential needs," based on what you learned by drawing out your matrix.

You, the Sales Manager, will be driving your Sales Reps to success that they deserve and will continue to support throughout their careers. Its one thing to hand out leads, but when they take on "Golden Nuggett" Status you won't be able to stop them from knocking the cover off the ball. Our Seattle Branch Conference Room Walls were covered with reams of charts allowing each Sales Rep access to a host of valuable "Hot" information based on a referral outlining the successes that we were already having in a similar business or department within a business.

Type of Product	$ Value Of The Sale	Zip Code Numbers	SIC/ NAICS Code	Survey Date Completed	Demo Date Complete

COLUMN 6 - DOLLAR VALUE OF THE SALE

This is another vital piece of information for you to review because of the multiple effect the dollar value triggers throughout the entire sales process. Depending upon the maturity and tenure of the sales rep, you need to review this early in the process to insure that the Customer has been presented with the very best alternative not only to meet their present requirements, but also future needs.

New sales reps have a tendency to sell toward the lower price; they do this because they believe it is an easier path to beating the competition. However, this is

**Dollar Value
of the Sale**

short sighted because it doesn't always provide the best solution to the Customer in terms of the challenges they face: remember you and your reps always want to know how it will increase revenues for the Customer, how it will be more convenient and make their lives easier.

The cost of a single sale may not appear competitive, but if taken over the course of time and additional orders, this reality might change. Make sure your reps are not always just comparing apples to apples. Look from a different perspective. While your product may be slightly more costly on a small order, it may be vastly less expensive in the long run, or in larger quantities than the completion, or even in a different "application" either in that department or another. That is stating the obvious I realize, but it should give you pause for other comparisons such as delivery times, delivery costs, ease of use, etc. There are many ways you can dif-ferentiate yourself without comparing apples to apples.

Personally, I always dug deep in this area even into my personal relationships with my Customers. As you just read in the previous section, there is a lot to be said for something as simple as constantly providing insights and ideas to your Customers by sending them articles, books, notes and emails on big news in their industry. I always felt that if I couldn't compete on price one order at a time, no one worked harder or longer than I did to provide "added value" to my Customer's experience. In other words, I always tried to exceed their expectations. There is a hidden value here that only you and your Customers understand, one that the competition is most likely aware of or practicing—just a thought.

As I said earlier, is the sales rep asking: What's in it for my Customer? What are the Customers chances for success? Using this column will help uncover all sorts of weaknesses in the sales rep's approach that can be changed quickly.

In the rush to complete an 80/20 program at a business the following occurred. The business deleted a product *type* because total sales for this one product were extremely low. Nobody looked at the Customer who was the principal buyer of this product for what else they purchased ($500M + per year.) The Customer placed their usual once a year order for this one unique, low volume product due to a job they had every year and when they found out that we had discontinued this one product type they simply contacted a competitor and got a quote which was lower in price than what they had presently been paying. The competitor recognized the opportunity or the gap we'd left and within a few months had captured the majority of the $500M business we had been doing annually for a very long period of time. Truly a major blunder.

Dollar Value of the Sale

Too many businesses follow trends such as the 80/20 rule. They claim that 80% of their business (generally speaking) is from 20% of their Customers and that those Customers who *only* buy small quantities of a certain product should be deleted because they don't contribute enough to the bottom line.

Please be very careful if you do this. Don't overlook the Customer in terms of what they are buying in *total* from your business, and just focus on the low sales of this one product. Don't overlook the value of a referral that may be a far larger Customer, or just another Customer to add to your bottom line.

The lesson is not to judge a Customer by a single product purchase or even the dollar value of that one product. Investigate, think bigger and see the big picture. Don't allow the dollar value of the sale by itself dictate the approach to any business.

$ Value Of The Sale	Zip Code Numbers	SIC/ NAICS Code	Survey Date Completed	Demo Date Completed	Propo Prep D

COLUMN 7 - ZIP CODE NUMBERS

Those beautiful five digits were a Godsend to sales reps when the U.S. Postal Service so graciously developed them. They are extremely valuable. Here's just one example: A zip code tells you the geographical area for the sales reps territory, which provides an enormous amount of hidden information such as: types of business concentrations in that area, environmental structure, type of mobility for your reps and much, much more.

For instance, here is an example many sales managers overlook: in a densely populated downtown or urban environment, a sales rep can park his or her car in a central location and walk the territory easily. This is far more efficient than a zip code that is more spread out that requires the sales rep to be getting into or out of his or her vehicle continuously. Knowing the proper zip codes can also eliminate potentially difficult parking problems since they tell you all the business types in that area.

A lack of this kind of information can waste incredible amounts of time and of course, the number of prospects a sales rep can reach in a day.

Combining Zip codes with NAICS codes also tell us where the concentration of prospects are, they identify what types are in that code and also what types are not in that code. The sales rep has to know his territory by zip codes intimately. It is also interesting to note that often, various types of companies such as manufacturing, medical supplies, restaurants, etc., tend to cluster together more than apart. This would be particularly true for restaurants that feed off each other's proximity. If you were a restaurant supply sales person, this information would be particularly useful in a new unfamiliar territory.

You, as the new sales manager need to observe which parts of the territory the sales rep is planning to work by day and week to insure maximum time in front of potential prospects. A map will help determine these areas for, "Behind the windshield time exposure." You can generate a quick listing of the top five Customer types currently being served and then plot out concentrations of potential prospects in this territory to help the sales rep work a sector correctly resulting in maximization of time. Zip codes do most of the work for you.

When working in the field, you should expect your sales reps to be in front of potential Customers 80%

of the time and driving or walking 20% of the time. Without using this kind of Zip code information, the opposite could be true. This concept applies even more for reps who must travel longer distances by air.

Column eight data covering SIC & NAICS codes (coming up) will contribute greatly to effective territory coverage.

Your Customer base should always be arranged by zip codes. In addition, get a printout of SIC/NAICS codes, type of products sold and total sales revenues. If you can manipulate this data, you will have a virtual gold mine that you can use with your sales reps.

Here is an example of what the zip code areas represented in the Des Moines branch of my company at the time: We knew that education represented our major Customers but we didn't know the level of concentration in certain geographic areas; yet these areas were far from penetrated in that there were still many educational facilities that weren't using our systems. On the other hand, we identified those zip codes that were not educationally geared; these were primarily farms. State government was our largest business with a broad placement of equipment and supplies, yet an analysis revealed that we had a spotty effort across a number of State Government Agencies. However, it was interesting to see that this branch did approximately 65% of their business in education and government. Local and federal government agencies represented less than 10% of our business, which was primarily coming from USDA agencies.

During a branch meeting, I asked the question about placements in our traditional markets where our strengths were very evident, which were: accounting, legal, architects, and engineering. The sales reps indicated that we were doing business with all the accountants in the State Capitol. We took a quick look and found out that we were doing business with only

18 firms. There were 97 accountants listed in the zip codes covering the State capital area. The silence in the room was deafening. We then proceeded to analyze lawyers (which had always been a huge market for us), which showed an even lesser penetration.

We reviewed the key five factors as well as groups and geographical concentrations—how much of the territory was in one area. We identified trending and key applications and successes in each market. Finding out which applications were appropriate was now a challenge to every sales rep.

From that moment on, our Des Moines branch was one of the fastest growing operations in the Midwest region. The other key city in the Des Moines branch territory was Lincoln/Omaha center for which we did the same analysis.

Success breeds success. Our TTR made this happen every day. Des Moines had the lowest turnover rate of any branch in the country—is it any wonder? Capture that zip code information in this column and combine it with the NAICS code and USE IT to create a constant flow of success driven leads.

$ Value Of The Sale	Zip Code Numbers	SIC/ NAICS Code	Survey Date Completed	Demo Date Completed	Propos Prep D

COLUMN 8 - SIC / NAICS CODES

Following on the heels of the previous discussion, these two codes are perhaps the most underutilized management/sales tools available to you. They can provide immediate direction to a wide variety of business opportunities in any specific territory or national locations. If you can identify the SIC/NAICS codes where your product is serving Customer requirements, then you can also identify additional suspects simply by geographically identifying "like" SIC/NAICS codes and then grouping them effectively.

Your marketing department can perform most of their functions in generating products, place, price, and promotion as well by using the data that this code provides. I'm sure they know that, but have they shared it with you?

The specific direction provided by Marketing can be driven by the applications developed by the sales rep that provide solutions/benefits as well.

You need to wear two hats in this respect, as you will also be a mini-Marketing Manager in territory coverage. The TTR report provides you with a valuable tool by having the sales rep provide either of these codes for the prospect. It opens the doors to the immediate and highly effective way of generating information on businesses that are most likely to behave like your "best Customers." What a powerful tool for you!

Since the beginning of the decade, the NAICS code has been more flexible than the SIC codes due to having six digits instead of four that are available in the

SIC codes. This makes their content more specific and detailed. Both codes are still in effect, however any new users should use the NAICS code. It is relatively easy to make a conversion from SIC codes; there are numerous crossover aids to provide assistance to those businesses that might be using the SIC code.

The SIC/NAICS codes represent a treasure trove that you have constant access to, but you must use it! It is estimated that 40% of the businesses in America don't use this valuable tool. All that is needed is for the sales rep to enter the applicable code for the prospect and the immediate evaluation of the size and type of business will be made during the next One-on-One session. This is an automatic referral list just waiting for you to use. Just identify the codes for the Customers you're already serving and go after new ones in the same codes! I told you the TTR makes it all so simple.

The sales rep doesn't even have to close the deal to allow everyone to maximize the *applications information*. The rep need only identify the businesses through the codes that have a high probability of needing your products and services. That's a powerful strategy that is available to every sales manager and it puts the sales reps in the enviable position of never having to make a "cold" call again! In addition, we all know few sales people enjoy cold calling. Have them instead make hot calls based on the knowledge that they will gain from getting information from you; One-on-One management in action to create a win-win oriented environment using the readily available NAICS data by the sales rep. How much simpler can it get?

Make your reps use the TTR constantly and tout the great value it has to everyone in increasing their individual effectiveness and incomes. Teach them to use it to their own benefit as you use it together.

You will now be forced to work closely with the Marketing area to maximize the opportunity that is afforded to your company by the effective use of SIC/NAICS codes. However, you should not be expected to do the work of Marketing. Your main responsibility is to supply information that reflects what is happening in the field such as applications information and SIC/NAICS codes and of course always informing Marketing about the likes, dislikes and questions your Customers may have about your products and or services.

It is the responsibility of Marketing to generate additional support by exploring the success of sales with numerous databases, direct mail, social networks, trade shows, trade association exposure, publicity releases, and numerous additional sources. In addition, Marketing can do some basic but valuable work in the area of breaking down the SIC/NAICS codes by geography, annual sales, number of employees or by dozens of other vital marketing indicators for use by both of your departments.

Every existing and potential Customer will have either a SIC or a NAICS code or both. The codes will provide the road to success by finding the type of businesses that have an application for your equipment and total capabilities; and matching their SIC/NAICS code to all the identical businesses in the entire territory.

You can drive knowledge about any business and its location by using these codes. Databases and directories carry these codes and they can be arranged by several key factors.

A brief description of the NAICS code structure

NAICS (North American Industry Classification System) is used by business and government to classify "business establishments" according to type of economic activity (Process of Production) in Canada, Mexico and the United States of America.

An establishment is generally a *physical* location where business is conducted or where services or industrial operations are performed. An enterprise, on the other hand, may consist of more than one location performing the same or different types of economic activities. Each establishment in that enterprise is assigned a NAICS code based on its own primary business activity and physical location.

The NAICS numbering system employs six digits at the most detailed industry level. The first five digits are generally the same in all three countries. You can utilize the code for a variety of sales applications by focusing on any of the following segments:

1. First two digits designate the largest business sector
2. Third digit designates the sub-sector
3. Fourth digit indicates the industry
4. Fifth digit designates the NAICS industry (Key to most analysis)
5. Sixth digit designates the national industries

SIC / NAICS
Codes

I strongly recommend that you utilize all resources within your business to implement the use of NAICS codes with all your Customers in Canada, Mexico and most importantly the United States. For those sales managers doing business in countries that are not covered by NAICS, I will be blogging out information on other sources of key industry information in my future communications.

In addition, as I said, I have always had great success using the research librarians at public libraries. These people have unknowingly made me a lot of money. They helped me identify the SIC/NAICS codes for an account that I had just sold and then helped me identify the same SIC/NAICS codes for other businesses in my territory. What a fantastic tool! By using the Research Librarian, you don't even have to buy the databases; why would I buy expensive data bases, when I have free access to every Major Data Base at the Schaumburg, Illinois Library? As a matter of fact I can access these data bases online from anywhere.

The Marketing Department can identify exactly how many identical businesses are there and their geographical concentrations. Add in the power of the miracle that took place in that sale and the applications that contributed to generating revenues and profits for Customers, and you have empowered that list of potential prospects for your sales reps.

This is the area that presently represents the biggest SILO effect in most businesses. Marketing is making all the sales decisions and sales managers are acting like puppets on a string. The one major strength that the sales team has, is access to the Customer, so the sales manager should position himself as a collaborative implementer of customer applications and observations with whatever department within the company he or she can form a mutually satisfying alliance.

Until the sales manager gets to working with Marketing, it is doubtful that the Marketing SILO will be doing much to generate the leads and providing the support that the sales manager and rep deserve. It is a terrible thing to say, but the sales manager often has to become the Marketing Manager for his sales reps and make things happen to a degree that Marketing will want to become involved, and they will, it's always just a matter of time.

As you begin to use this valuable tool, you'll begin to get numerous SIC/NAICS codes from your sales reps placing more and more prospects on the TTR report!

As noted a minute ago in my own experience, your Research Librarians are your best assistants (and they are free). And don't forget to recognize their contributions at important times in the year with small tokens of your appreciation.

Yes, I know today's technology offers up incredible search engine capabilities and those should also be used of course, but nothing really beats a visit to your local library and a smile for the Research Librarian who generally loves his or her work and is eager to help you. (If possible you should try to arrange one of your sales meetings at a Library where a Research Librarian can introduce and explain all the capabilities that are available to the sales reps.)

$ Value Of The Sale	Zip Code Numbers	SIC/ NAICS Code	Survey Date Completed	Demo Date Completed	Propos Prep D

COLUMN 9 - SURVEY-DATE COMPLETED

No matter how short, long or detailed a survey is, the sales rep has to be able to justify the need for the product by the Customer. Varying industries will have different Survey requirements but the essential need is for data to justify a real need and to put that in quantifiable terms.

If your product can't provide savings in time, money or put your Customer in a better competitive position, it is highly unlikely that you have a prospect!

We want to avoid making judgments about the numerous businesses that might have varying survey points that need answering. Therefore, I apologize for avoiding descriptors, but we do know one universal fact: if a written justification/proposal is required, your rep and you must have quantifiable data/information.

This Survey date precedes the date of becoming a real prospect. Early in the sales process, a rep will have to identify a need that can be quantified and justified: What's in it for the customer? What are their chances of success? Without identifying a need the sales rep will have failed the first question in the prospect qualifier and most likely will not be able to continue the sales process. If the rep can't answer these two questions, you will have to alter the strategy as to continuing calls on this business.

You may be unable to create the Survey Questions that will apply to every business; however, there are three sources of knowledge about a sales opportunity. First is that the Customer reveals that they have a need. Second is experience with similar Customers in the same industry. Third, is knowledge from the sales reps that comes as a result doing their "homework" and applying a high degree of creativity. Combining these three critical sources will assure that by employing a highly structured questionnaire that confirms the existence or non-existence of a need for your equipment or services, they will be on the right track for a sale.

Having completed a Survey on a specific date and established that there is a need sets a time line that justifies the start of the closing steps of the sales cycle and measures how quickly the suspects *don't* play a role.

A simple Survey also measures how quickly the suspect was converted to a prospect and the relative early strength of the intention to buy your product.

This can be utilized by you when working with the rep in analyzing the quality and addition of suspects from the pipeline. This is also why the sales rep should track the suspect on a TTR report form to allow for an organized and uniform approach to tracking suspects *and* prospects.

Leaving the tracking of suspects to 10 different approaches will result in additional time wasted in the critical area of building and maintaining a viable pipeline. Note: This use of a TTR report that monitors suspects is only a recommendation; prospects represent the only accountable factors that will be tracked by you with the report.

Here are some other valuable thoughts about the survey process:

1. What benefits can your products or services provide over the systems used currently by the Customer?

2. What features of their present system do they like the most—the least?

3. What time frames are involved in completing the average job, and how many jobs per hour/day/week are being performed?

4. Would the Customer acquire a new system if your rep could show them significant increases in productivity, which could be translated to lower prices, superior Customer service, higher profits, and other key factors?

5. Does the Customer have the budget available to acquire this equipment or service?

6. Is the sales rep's contact the final Decision Maker? This is the time to get a clear definition of the affected areas both positive/negative and a clear identification of the personnel and their titles in the approval matrix. Getting this information will contribute greatly to understanding the total environment in which the sales rep will be operating.

Answering these questions will start the justification process to make sure that this suspect has earned the right to appear on the TTR report as a prospect. If the sales rep is not completing a Survey that will provide the above information at a minimum, they will not be placing that suspect on the TTR. This clearly raises red flags for you. You must remind the rep that the path to least resistance is a path to destruction. You are the only person who can remove a prospect from the TTR. However, removal will not take place without in-depth discussions with the sales rep. This step will avoid the disappearance of prospects unless every resource has been exhausted.

As I grew in my sales experience, the element of establishing trust played a major part in the survey step. I learned that you must deal with a suspect in a very business-like manner—the rep must stop *visiting* and start getting the permission to complete the Survey with a promise that when they are done, they will be reviewing the Survey data with the Decision Maker to make sure that they fully understand what the Customer wanted and needed.

This process is very much like when I call the cable company with a problem. The first thing their rep says to me after I've explained my problem is: "I hear what you've said so let's make sure I understand you correctly." Then he goes on to repeat my request.

You want your sales reps to be thorough, precise, and well prepared with all the people they will work with in every phase of the sale. Most of that information comes from your Customers. The rep wants to convey clearly to them that she understands them as well as their systems and challenges they are trying to improve or solve. After all, this step will represent the present method section of their proposal that will result in the proposed solution. These solutions must result in a savings of money, increased productivity or some other key benefits. Unless you can impact revenue and profitability in numerous ways, your chances for a sale will be minimized.

Two questions that should be answered before the sales starts:

1. Does the survey include a solution that satisfies the prospect's needs
2. Who other than the prospect will be involved in the final decision?

Through the survey step, the rep should be insuring that they are also making every effort to identify the other 4.4 Decision Makers who will be receiving their proposed solution and should feel that the rep is including the other decision maker's best interests in this endeavor too.

The rep's efforts if properly done, will translate into 4.4 additional "economic sellers" (as near to clones as the rep is likely to get) because he or she will make them realize that by selling for you, they will be selling for themselves because the rep will be adding to their values as they see greater and faster returns.

The rep's questions should be centered on whatever impact their product or system can have on the prospect's business. In essence, improved profits become the sales rep's product. In fact, this is worth repeating: the Customer's product is also your sales rep's products. Along with providing added value and exceeding expectations, the best attitude and approach is for your sales reps to affect, but more importantly internalize "ownership" of that Customer's products, along with that Customer's concerns, worries, angst and successes! Be the Customer. Be the product. Be the Customer's Customers!

For all these reasons the sales reps will need to conduct this survey to quantify the benefits that will accrue to the prospect's business.

$ Value Of The Sale	Zip Code Numbers	SIC/ NAICS Code	Survey Date Completed	Demo Date Completed	Propos Prep D

COLUMN 10 - DEMO - DATE COMPLETED

If your product requires a demonstration, your sales reps need to make sure the following four criteria are addressed:

1. Have the key people attend the demonstration. Most important is to have the people who will actually be using your product in attendance. This is vital because too often we see sales reps invite Decision Makers who have little involvement in the actual use of the product. Often, this is where the sale is lost because users simply won't use your process for whatever un stated reason/s, or the user simply likes his

present supplier and isn't in the mood to change. Remember, you and your reps are unique in the corporate world because you are in the 5% club—those sales professionals who understand Golde's Rule #1. Refer to the organizational chart earlier in this book. Push the Customer to the top of that pyramid and put all the SILOS at the bottom. Understand that many of the Decision Makers in the 5.4 count have practically no involvement with their own Customers, much as what might be happening in your own company.

2. The best location to perform a demo is in an existing satisfied Customer's location. Every sales manager like yourself needs to develop one of these "satisfied Customers" who will help you conduct a demo and answer the prospect's questions if that prospect is in the same business. Regardless of whether they are, they can still promote you in general. With video and teleconferencing, it is easy to

organize numerous demo approaches

3. Every sales rep should have numerous video demos available on his or her smartphone or tablet. Those demos should reside right next to the testimonial videos we already spoke about. This allows him or her to move the process from suspect to prospect more quickly and in such a vivid and animated way

4. You need to work closely with Marketing to coordinate this effort and have their support to make these demos readily available to you. There is nothing like listening and seeing a satisfied Customer tell "your" story better than you can

Without being able to support your product with a benefits oriented demo in whatever format that your sales rep can implement, it is highly unlikely that a rapid close will take place. The demo can range from a brief video available on mobile devices, as e-mail on the computer, or in the showroom, but by far the most effective demo is the one conducted at a satisfied user's (one of your other Customer's) location.

Depending on the product and the overall implications involved, any of these demo types should be used as a proof statement as quickly as possible. The point at which a potential Customer raises objections should be your cue to turn that into a benefit by showing him or her your demo. If your sales rep is unable to overcome the objection at the demo, or even some-what later, there is no reason to continue the process unless your sales rep can trade off those objections with other benefits you have to offer. This is usually the point in the sales process that starts providing a clear indication of the strength, weakness, or futility of talking to Decision Makers any further.

Proposal Prep Date	Proposal Presentation & Review	Date For Follow Up	Date For Follow Up	Date For Follow Up	Forcast Closin Date

COLUMN 11 - PROPOSAL PREPERATION DATE

The proposal is a document that is often confused with a "price quote."

It is not a quote!

You need to prepare for it.

A sales rep often feels they don't need a proposal because they've already done the necessary work with videos and demonstration literature, and they are already dealing with the Decision Maker. Most don't understand (as stated here often) that there are an average of 4.4 people in B2B sales that are additionally involved beyond the actual decision maker—the one who approves the purchase.

The proposal serves as a sales rep on your behalf just as much as the video demo does. Without a proposal, you are leaving the responsibility of selling your product or service to your Decision Maker and the other 4.4 people who may not even truly be Decision Makers, but who want to appear to be that to your sales rep. Is it any wonder that the rep experiences so many delays closing the sale? Imagine the power struggles between the various "princes" in their various "fiefdoms" and the true roles these quasi Decision Makers play in approving a request to acquire your product?

Now, imagine the sales rep's contact having at his or her fingertips an electronic or paper proposal that they can distribute instantaneously to the other 4.4 colleagues. Through this very efficient path, your sales rep would be answering all the questions that could be objections for these individuals. The proposal represents a written document that provides justification for the content and answers the question of, "What's in it for the Customer?" and provides that answer in a form that requires action now!

You will need to prepare a proposal more than 90% of the time if you are to have any confidence in the fact that the Decision Maker will not be the person consummating the sale internally. They may not be qualified to do so, which may be the very thing that keeps delaying or torpedoing the sale. You need to make sure that every resource in the business is presented a proposal. The key focus is that you don't know how many internal Decision Makers there are. A Proposal helps you anticipate and answer any possible objections from any Decision Makers before you waste more time.

Later, I will provide a more in-depth insight into the vital role that the Proposal plays in making the sale. One early key, is to compare the time that has passed from the date of demo until the Proposal is prepared. The questions by you have to address any protracted delay between these vital dates. Why was there a delay? How could this time frame have been shortened?

The following steps should be part of every Proposal:

1. Introduction Letter: This should be no more than a two-page summary of the sales rep's concept of the work and his interest in submitting this Proposal because of the rewarding value presentation. It should begin with a compelling statement in order to encourage the reader to continue. This can be unusual, entertaining, or downright astounding. Whatever it is, it must be addressed personally

to the target or targets and it must contain a promise. The content of that promise is up to your rep. The sales rep should thank all the areas that helped in preparing this proposal with special emphasis on areas that will play a key role in the approval matrix. The letter should also include a strong closing statement setting the stage for readers to expect to be granting their approval for this acquisition. Begin and end in a compelling and memorable manner and if possible, add some urgency to the request for the sale. Be creative here—a time limit, an added bonus for early signing; anything that is dignified and believable

2. Table of Contents

3. Introduction to your business: Introduce total overall capabilities of your business to include key information about revenues, profits, number of employees, products, markets served and the most important contributor to the success of our business—the Customers

4. Customer is King or Queen: Your mission statement contains the commitment "That Your Success Is Our Success." This reflects a high degree of the important role of the Customer. Your organizational chart is one of the few in the industry that shows the Customer is on top being served by your entire organization starting with the CEO on the bottom pushing every layer of employee in the company towards a total collaborative effort to serve the Customer

By turning the traditional organizational chart upside down and putting the Customer on top, you will be introducing a revolutionary concept: the Customer appears in your organizational chart!

While most of the effective organizations we see try never to lose sight of who actually works for whom, they don't show that publicly in their commitments;

internal "princes in their fiefdoms" that have their own agendas generally hinder them

1. Present Method: This reflects the details of the methodology being used currently by the Customer as revealed by the work done by you during the survey step of the process. It is important to focus on methods that we can improve, but at the same time we should not be overlooking any areas no matter how small if we can show in the proposed method how our solution improves that situation

2. Proposed Method: Outline in detail the solutions that your system will bring to the Customer. These must be aimed at improving key areas outlined in the present method area

3. Comparison of Present vs. Proposed System Costs

4. Summary of Benefits: List all the benefits (both tangible and intangible) that will accrue to the Customer. It is here that you try to include the 5.4 average areas involved in the Decision Maker's approval matrix. The balancing act is to represent the benefits that will accrue to the total business, yet make an effort to highlight those areas that are key to the approval matrix

Wherever you can quantify savings generated by implementing the proposed solution and present them in a dollar comparison, you will have powerful evidence to support the question: What's in it for them? Highlight additional savings because of your ability to provide creative solutions such as financing, leasing, etc.

5. Installation and Training: Outline the specific steps and schedules for the installation and training of key personnel

6. Technical Service: Stress the importance of all types of technical or other types of support that will insure 24/7 operation and ability to access help as required

7. Customer service: Some examples of specific functions Customer service would perform are: scheduled calls, automatic replenishment of supplies once timing and/or usage has been established

8. Schedule on-going follow-up visits by the sales rep and a highly qualified Customer Service Department to handle requirements on a Customer oriented demand schedule

9. Referrals: List all the referral accounts like Customers that are currently enjoying the benefits of meeting and exceeding their goals due to use of your system. The more referrals for which you can provide an account name the more specific value you will be adding. However, should you not be able to, or want

to, disclose Customer names, you can discuss the applications in detail and mention the total number of Customers served in that industry. The key is to make this section of the proposal as powerful as possible

10. Exhibits: Include a series of exhibits that would be required to provide lengthy information most often related to product and performance specifications. Graphs should be included wherever they could make it easier to understand due to a visual emphasis

11. Order Form: A completed order form should be included with every proposal copy listing all the bottom line costs that would be involved in covering all the system components

12. And last, but certainly not least: The appearance of your proposal (in the tangible hand held version) should be as professional as possible. This means it may be necessary to enlist any in-house designer capabilities or if you

utilize an outside advertising agency, they can do this work. Always pretend that you are competing with a Fortune 1000 company and never, ever forget, "You never get a second chance to make a first impression." The cover of the proposal is an equalizer that you can make you look as good or even better than your largest competitor

You have to utilize the power of the Proposal in as many situations as possible since the sales rep has to realize that increasing that power at least six times the average is necessary in every B2B sale.

The value proposition has to be evaluated to be sure that it is always stated in Customer terms. These terms have to be quantified where possible to provide assurance to the Customer that his or her advantage lies in increasing revenues and lowering costs rather than descriptions of the operating specifications that only yields them features.

A key factor that must be cited is the competitive advantage that will result from the use of your system. Special attention should be focused on key approval matrix areas that will benefit from being more competitive. Your system has to multiply a budget's funds by putting in more than they take out through returning a higher yield to the budgets available

Proposal Prep Date	Proposal Presentation & Review	Date For Follow Up	Date For Follow Up	Date For Follow Up	Forcast Closin Date

COLUMN 12 - PROPOSAL PRESENTATION & REVIEW

This date is important to you because it generates questions to the sales rep that address the Who, How, How many, Why's and If's that the rep needs.

1. Was the order closed?
2. Who was the proposal presented to?
3. How many people were in attendance?
4. Who were the additional persons attending the presentation and their titles?
5. Did any additional objections arise that the sales rep could not answer right there?
6. If the order was not closed at this important meeting, did the sales rep find out specifics of

why not and get a commitment that if the answer to meet and overcome the objection takes place that the order will be placed?

This is an important step at this point because you don't want to lose that fish that the rep has on the hook

7. If additional proof/information is required, the sales rep should get as much of the specifics at this point as possible

8. At this point, the rep will be thankful that all the information is in a professionally prepared written Proposal that takes over the role of the Internal Sales Representative, and one for which numerous copies will have to be available to be left behind or transmitted electronically. That leaves the selling control still in the sales reps hands as the Proposal keeps working while he or she is not there to present to additional approval sources.

Proposal Presentation

1. Attendees: The sales rep should make every attempt to have as many of the approval matrix players be in attendance at the presentation. With extensive video capabilities, you might have to make a conference call presentation. It might be an easier way to get a decision if more than one decision maker needs to be involved. We are well aware of the 4.4 factor. The same requirements will be required as if you were making a person-to-person presentation.

2. Audio Visual: The proposal contents should be presented on a screen wherever possible to maintain the attention of the attendees. They should be informed that the sales rep will provide a copy of the proposal at the conclusion of the presentation.

3. Keys to Presentation With You In Attendance:

   (a) You, as sales manager to make sure the audiovisual or video conferencing details are in place and working. A quick run through the presentation prior to meeting would be recommended

   (b) Make sure the sales rep stops at the end of each major or series of points and asks if there are any questions

   (c) If a question can't be answered, you should make a note and promise to get the answer. You nor the sales rep should try to guess or provide a questionable answer. Just say that you don't have the answer to that but that the rep will get it to them within 24 hours

   (d) At the end of the presentation each attendee should be provided with a copy of the proposal

4. Close: Are there any additional questions? Once there are no more questions, the sales rep has to ask for the order by asking the decision maker to sign the completed order form that accompanies every Proposal

5. The following question should be asked (if there is not an approval of the proposal): "Can you share your reason for not approving the order today?" In a B2B situation you've done a lot of work getting to this point including a demonstration and a proposal. You have essentially wrestled a fish in the water and brought it up to the rails of the boat. At this point, you don't want to let up on the pole without getting an answer to that question.

Too often I have seen the sales effort disappear because some lower Decision Maker came up with an off-the-wall objection that stopped the whole process

The Sales Manager (if present) should be interceding on behalf of his employee and asking some of the key questions. You and your rep have to uncover the reason for the delay in closing and then provide the corrective action to overcome that objection and do it quickly so that you don't experience more than one follow-up call. However, this is not always the case in a retail setting. For example, a high end automobile salesperson might not push with a question like this. He or she hasn't necessarily invested the kind of time on a preliminary "walk on" prospect as your sales rep typically does in a B2B sale. Selling a Mercedes would generally take more time to develop a relationship. However, in a B2B setting, the rep often invests a great deal of time in the kinds of things we've been talking about including research, proposals, etc., and so he or she has a right to ask the question: Can you share your reason for not approving this order today? He or she deserves a commitment or at least a good reason why the sale cannot be closed today. Your sales rep can help the prospect with his or her answer by asking questions like: Is there any information missing in my proposal that would help you make a decision? Do any of the other Decision Makers need more information?

6. Proposal Appearance: (See previous page again as well.) The proposal should be commensurate with the level of your largest competitor. This could make the difference. Especially, if you have a high quality proposal cover that shows an impressive image and a powerful logo plus an imprint on the spine. Remember that some of the Decision Makers will not have met the sales rep. All they will have to go on will be the Proposal. The Proposal will be your silent sales rep; as close to a clone of you as you might get

The proposal should be reviewed by you whenever possible to make sure that every feature, benefit, answer, and potential objection is included. This is done through the process of collaboration by everyone in your business to ultimately serve the Customer but should begin with a One-on-One conversation with your rep.

Collaboration is often over used to the point where it loses its true meaning. You need to recognize where your sales reps stand in that process. A copy of the proposal should be created to distribute to every employee in your business. You never know where a great idea might come from. Fresh eyes are paramount, especially with very large potential clients.

The reason for this is obvious; when preparing the proposal, every single area of your business should be involved and should contribute as required. As a matter of fact, the standard pages outlining the key areas of the business should be printed and designed by a good graphic artist if possible. The variable pages should be prepared by your sales rep and should fit the overall proposal. Even the cover should be designed for optimal effectiveness to provide the impression that the Customers will be served by a well-oiled machine.

The only way to overcome the internal barriers that exist within every prospect is through preparing and presenting a well thought out, shared, powerful, and all-inclusive proposal. Professionally prepared proposals will help you level the playing field. Obviously, the sales rep should use this to close if the Decision Maker is really the true decision maker. You'll quickly realize if your sales rep has invited the key personnel to the proposal presentation if only a limited number of personnel attend other than the key main contact. If this happens, it will result in no decision being made at the presentation. This is a red flag that not all the 5.4 Decision Makers have seen the proposal.

In my sales activity I was closing slowly because I was working closely with my Decision Maker reporting to him key dates that I had gathered during the survey step. He accepted the data and thanked me along with setting a definite next step. However, I missed the fact that there were 4.4 other Decision Makers.

That is the purpose of a well-prepared proposal. The proposal is your silent sales rep that is selling 24/7 and your product is getting the maximum exposure. (You could also apply this thinking to the resume you are going to send before you get to this point.) Especially if you know the other 4.4 Decision Makers and can tailor their own copy with the benefits that will accrue to them. A great professional proposal is a tool that will differentiate you from the competition.

Most of the contents of the proposal can be prepared in a professional manner so that the sales rep only has to add the variable information such as general information names, present method, proposed method, comparison of methods, cost factors, summary of benefits, etc. This translates to 80-90% already being there which results in the sales rep having to add 10-20% of variable content. Marketing should be in charge of preparing the dedicated proposal information.

All of this information because you simply filled in a date for when the Proposal was due, which led to a One-on-One conversation or series of conversations! Amazing.

Proposal Prep Date	Proposal Presentation & Review	Date For Follow Up	Date For Follow Up	Date For Follow Up	Forcast Closin Date

Dates of Added Follow-Up

COLUMN 13, 14, 15 - DATES OF ADDED FOLLOW-UP

At this point, you should be communicating and offering assistance in whatever form required. The sales reps should be making these calls, but if they feel that they will not be closing, they need to feel comfortable enough to level with you when they need help. If you've established a strong One-on-One relationship with your rep, this will be easy and will happen as a matter of course. The longer the delay in closing and increasing the number of follow-up calls, the more apparent something is amiss and you should get involved.

By now, everything I've told you, the ideas I've given you, the step by step manual of using the TTR, the examples of real experiences based on each column must now be sinking in; just how simple it is to create and maintain an extremely valuable dialogue with your reps—One-on-One with a single digital document, and how this translates to greater sales. Remember though, the magic is in how you use it and how often you use it. The even greater value of the TTR lies in its ability, through using it, to constantly help you create ideas, new paths to sales and further creative and critical thinking on your part and on the part of your sales reps.

These three columns are critical in measuring the progress of the sales process in the selling cycle.

		Forcasted Closing Date			
te For ow Up	Date For Follow Up	Forcasted Closing Date	Date Closed	Install And Training Date	Date Of Referral

COLUMN 16 - FORECASTED CLOSING DATE

The sales rep has to commit to a closing date during his initial eight steps that must precede all others in order to be a prospect."

The field for all the steps of the process takes place between the TTR date that started this whole sequence and the forecasted closing date. *Both of these dates manage the process;* they give you the information you need to guide your rep using the One-on-One Sales Management System. Missing steps while getting closer to the forecasted closing date should raise red flags and

be the impetus for serious strategy conversations between you and the rep.

This forecasted closing date was established when
the sales rep declared the business a prospect, a vital
step in getting the commitment of the sales rep to this
being a viable sales opportunity and one for which you
need to muster every resource available.

While you are focused on the five prospects added in a given month that were forecasted to close in
60-90 days, for example, with four forecasted in the
first 15 days of the month, we have to recognize that
the sales rep will have added prospects since then. As
these prospects are added, you need to be making every
effort to prioritize them by various factors of importance and provide the support to see if they can be
moved up to close faster than the usual closing cycle
time. Every effort should be made to constantly maintain a winning sense of urgency, which means that the

rep should always be closing someone! The question should be asked by you as to what it will it take to get these five orders to close on or before the forecasted date?

The key to this date is that the sales rep draws a line in the sand to let everyone know that an order can be expected between the date of becoming a Prospect and the forecasted closing date. The sales process has to be managed to make the close happen between these dates.

When both sales manager and rep see the importance of having a constant flow of prospects being added to the TTR, the One-on-One driven environment will become very evident. The reason for negative sales results in so many businesses is that we fail to recognize the fact that it starts and ends with the effectiveness of the sales manager in creating a One-on-One driven environment for success.

Date Closed

te For ow Up	Date For Follow Up	Forcasted Closing Date	Date Closed	Install And Training Date	Date Of Referral

COLUMN 17 - DATE CLOSED

This date measures the effectiveness of the sales rep in meeting and exceeding the forecasted closing date. There will come a point in the development of the sales rep when you will be able to take their forecasted sales to the bank, the minute they become prospects and "get a loan" for the period in question. Once you establish a closing ratio for each sales rep, then you will be able to provide reliable forecasts that will increase the effectiveness and profitability of the total business.

te For ow Up	Date For Follow Up	Forcasted Closing Date	Date Closed	Install And Training Date	Date Of Referral

COLUMN 18 - DATE OF INSTALLATION & TRAINING

Often the sale starts at this point in the sales process. If the scheduled installation or delivery and training can't be close to the closing date, you must investigate the reasons behind any delays. It is unlikely that the Customer will pay the bill unless experiencing a satisfactory installation and training of personnel who will be working with the equipment or services. The longer the delay, the more chances for something to go wrong in ways that are sometimes unimaginable.

You have to stay very close to the sales rep to make sure that this urgency stays at the same level as the sale. It is not a sale until the Customer pays your bill!

te For ow Up	Date For Follow Up	Forcasted Closing Date	Date Closed	Install And Training Date	Date Of Referral

COLUMN 19 - DATE OF REFERRAL

This date is vital to the sales rep as well as you. If the Customer is willing to give you a positive referral regarding the benefits that are being derived from the use of your equipment or services, you have another powerful sales tool in your bag if you use it. The power of a neutral third party endorsement of you and your product and or services is incalculable.

You must teach your sales rep to use all of the endorsements you have when approaching new prospects. For this reason, you will have to insist that your sales reps get referrals at every opportunity. (We've already discussed the particulars of using video and pictures on their smartphones, etc.)

Most Customers, even those that are very satisfied, will not volunteer the time to do this, so your sales rep must ask for it! Nothing is ever lost by asking.

You have to actively promote voluntary cooperation as well as culture change in recognizing that referrals can be extremely productive in providing an easier way to develop Prospects.

Assume that a sales rep closes six Customers a month, and 33% of these provide a referral that yields one new prospect. That translates to 12 hot prospects a year or 120 prospects for all the 10 sales reps. That's 120 cold calls that don't have to be made. If you can impact that rate to increase to 50% of the closed sales that provide a referral that yields two prospects per month. Of course, the 10 sales reps will benefit from the doubling of the number to 240 a year or 20 per month!

It is only when the Customer is completely satisfied

with the product and or service that will you be paid, but more importantly will you begin to have the ability to use that Customer as a referral.

Referrals represent the most underused sales strategy employed today when it plays such an important role in maintaining your image with the Customer. Referrals are also part of the "Customer for life" philosophy I always employ. As an example, in the life insurance business, the very top tier sales agents make a good living off the rest of one policy holder's family and friends. Once that initial sale is made and booked, a good insurance salesman's job is just starting. The next question will be: How can I get referrals from John Doe and how can I get the phone numbers for all his family and friends?

The same holds true in real estate sales, where a "starter" home in the hands of a great sales person can be the seed that bears several, if not more sales, not only to the original buyer, but to everyone he or she knows.

We always concentrate on getting and closing the prospect but then fall down in these essential areas. We can be very good at helping our Customers find new uses for our products. We can be extremely good sales managers using the On-on-One techniques in this book. Our sales reps can be great at pointing out benefits and features, but the importance of referrals and lifetime sales cannot be overstated.

If the sales rep cannot obtain a referral in a written form, or use the installation as an actual demo site, this should raise a red flag that you need to explore with your sales rep. Why are we not getting a referral? There are many reasons why the Customer doesn't want to be used as a referral and that's okay. However, the all-important added value of a sale that everyone worked so hard on lies in referrals. Another question that must be answered is: What is the proper way to ask for a referral? There is no one proper way, there are dozens. It depends upon the intimacy of the relationship, how long the Customer has been satisfied and the mood of the Customer when the sales rep is about to broach the question. All in all however, this is a relatively straight forward question. I always chose to ask it in a comfortable setting, when the Customer was extremely happy with something I did for him. It's really as simple as writing or saying something along these lines:

"Mr. Doe (or John, if you are on more informal terms), I know that you are happy with our (products, services, etc.) because you've expressed that to me many times. I would like to be able to provide that same kind of service to my potential Customers. I wonder if I could ask you write up a very short statement as to how you liked our products, my service to you or anything else that is on your mind? As a matter of fact, knowing how busy you are, if you can give me an idea right now,

Date of Referral

I'd gladly write it out and then give it to you for your approval. We plan to use this in our newsletters."

In order to maximize the opportunity of every sale that has a unique application, you should explore the problem for which you and your sales rep provided the solution. You then look for every business that produces similar products and then provide a quick applications write up. You should then share this with your sales reps without any reference to that Customer because competitors don't need to know.

As the sales manager, you should have the knowledge of similar businesses. (SIC/NAICS) Codes will make that easy. Determining or having knowledge of these two facts will help you distribute leads. A new sales rep will get the smaller businesses and the larger business can be saved for when you work in the field with the new rep. As the sales manager working in One-on-One mode, you are not going to send a new sales rep into a large business for which you haven't provided direction or training. As a result of running a successful One-on-One Sales Management environment, this is a great opportunity to ask a developing sales rep who does have large account experience, to help.

There is one more benefit you will be providing in developing and sharing these applications; they will be used by various departments such as Marketing to build pride in the business, the products and the people.

Define referrals

A referral is when a person connects a business with another contact for creating a win-win situation for both parties. The key word in referrals is "trust." This is the factor that contributes to eliminating key uncertainties that block a sale in the early stages. Results from effective referrals indicate that using them builds momentum more quickly and significantly increases the closing rate. If a sales rep is not generating referrals on a consistent basis, a red flag should appear in the review of the TTR. (This should result in you checking on the sales activity that is attributed to this shortfall of referrals. You should expect at least a 50% rate of referrals from closed sales.)

The most effective referrals will come from people with whom the sales rep has established trust. If the answer to a request for a referral results in a definite no, then chances are great that the Customer isn't exhibiting trust in the business, the sales rep, and the equipment or services that they have purchased.

In today's viral world, negative input travels quickly. Therefore, you will have to prioritize your rep's inquiry into determining the status of the Customer. In the meantime, it is imperative for the sales rep to determine what steps need to be taken to correct this lack of a referral. In some cases it will just be a reason that focuses on a business process that the Customer does not want to expose due to not being in the best interests of their business. No matter what, you have to dig out the reason for a no, so you can overcome that objection in order to find out where you may have gone wrong and to then correct it. In fact, these kinds of action (rectifying a mistake) can often turn into even better referrals than you would have gotten in the first place.

A referral is not a referral until your source is willing to accept or write a note or make a phone call to put an action step in to play to share the success that they are experiencing with the installation and operation of your system, or until they allow you to publish their endorsement of you.

Besides getting referrals from new customers, who address the current state of your mutual capabilities, it is equally important not to overlook older Customers as an excellent source of referrals. Chances are that the "trust" factor is on a much firmer foundation and should result in actions such as on-site demos, video testimonials, and a clear statement regarding the favorable impact on revenue and profitability.

In addition, once the sales rep knows and understands the application that performed a "miracle" for the Customer, they should explore every area that could benefit from your systems to include other industries instead of just focusing on where you are having success.

We can always spot a strong sales rep as the one who is constantly talking about the miracles that his business can create and who is constantly passing out his business cards with the idea of seeking reciprocity in the terms of a new contact. These are the passionate ones who are your true brand fanatics.

Here is an interesting story about referrals that happened to me, what I called, "The unexpected referral."

During a field trip working with one of the sales reps in our Kansas City Branch at GBC, we were talking to one of the employees in the accounting office if she could refer us to someone inside the company that might be able to use one of our services or products (binder, binding, etc.). She said yes, she might and then she proceeded to tell us the story of her grandfather who had just passed away who had taught her the value of using the largest binders (3-inch spine) which he didn't need in terms of being able to accept the most documents possible as they related to his parts business.

She remembered her grandfather yelling at the sales people who tried to sell him 1-1/2 inch binders instead of the largest ones (3 or 4 inch) because the total number of pages dictated the smaller size. She related how he yelled about them not understanding his business. It turned out, he was absolutely correct from his own Customer's standpoint and here's why. From his very smart perspective, he saw the large binder as the least costly form of advertising that he could do with his Customers. Those large binders cost practically nothing in comparison to the continuing stream of repeat business he did with his Customers who had to use his binders for reference to buy his auto parts.

His competition used smaller binders, sometimes with only one-inch spines. His larger binders gave him more advertising "real estate" on which to print his company name, phone number, and logo much larger than anyone else's binders. To grandfather's mind, his binders were like cheap billboards shouting out his company name and phone number free.

When the parts people (his Customers) looked up on the shelf with all those little binders squeezed together with tiny type so small they couldn't be read from much further than two feet away, his binders jumped out all the way across the room with his phone number on the spine. In many cases, the ordering person just looked up from his desk, saw the number and dialed it.

The lesson to be learned here is to take every opportunity to ask for a referral. In this case, asking for the referral from the accounting woman turned into an opportunity to find another application for your products that will keep on giving for years to come.

Even today I see binder spines on shelves that have very small printing and leave lots of room that could be used for advertising, to draw the prospects due to ease of reading. Go into any architect's office and you'll see shelves of catalogs from various suppliers. Take a picture of those binders lining their shelves. Voila, you have a completely new list of suspects to call on, particularly the ones with the small binders. You can then call on all those suspects and offer them this same brilliant idea. Tell them the grandfather story. Tell them how their binders could be utilizing all that nearly empty space for large type advertising. Persuade them to switch to the larger binders or just provide the idea and get referred to the right contact for your product. Point out how this free advertising will increase their sales. This is the unexpected referral. In fact, you don't even have to ask for the referral, just take a picture and start making your calls.

In Closing

I think you can see through my tutorials and example stories that the One-on-One Sales Management System is as powerful as it is simple and easy to use. In fact, the power of the TTR is its simplicity and the many ways you can customize it to your needs. I could have included hundreds of other examples and stories in this book, but a word to the wise is usually sufficient. The real power of the TTR is the ideas you concur up on your own, given the examples I've presented. The possibilities are literally endless for a talented and driven sales manager.

In today's business world filled with the blessings and curses of technology, the egos and self-interests within our corporate organizations that continue to employ and rely on an archaic top down (CEO to Customer organization) structure and mentality, it is refreshing to know that there are those of you who just want to get the job done well, get it done right, and know the Customer is always at the top of the hierarchy.

You are the ones who will always find a way to be successful and to bring that success to your employers and the Shareholders and Customers who ultimately pay you. Now that you've taken on the role as the new Sales Manager, you get the chance to lead, mentor and manage One-on-One, the way things need to be structured in sales, the way things are done—simply and directly using your creativity and your years of experience.

It is time to be direct. It is time to take action to

reestablish the now nearly defunct rule that the Customer is King and Queen and always has been.

You've been wondering why your sales reps don't perform as well as you did…now you know but more importantly, you know how to fix it all.

I could have added a hundred other great stories about how to use each column in the TTR, but I have a feeling that since you bought this book, you already have plenty of your own ideas. I know you can see how this is not only a powerful instrument to measure success and/or catch potential failures before they hurt you, but it is a tool to become a commanding mentor to your sales reps.

As you can see by some of my stories, it is also an idea starter, a tracking device like no other, a way to simplify what in most cases today is an unnecessarily complicated way of doing business in the sales world.

Use this TTR as the tool that focuses your day. It as the face of One-on-One Sales Management will become indispensable and you'll wonder how you ever got along without it. Thank you for reading my book. I hope you will implement the One-on-One Sales Management System starting tomorrow at your own company.

For more information and timely updates and inspirations, visit my website at:

www.littleredsalesbook.com

Notes